Growing a caring
church

Published by
The Bible Reading Fellowship
15 The Chambers, Vineyard
Abingdon OX14 3FE
United Kingdom
Tel: +44 (0)1865 319700
Email: enquiries@brf.org.uk
Website: www.brf.org.uk

ISBN 978 1 84101 799 0

First published 2010
10 9 8 7 6 5 4 3 2 1 0
All rights reserved

Acknowledgments

Unless otherwise stated, scripture quotations are taken from the Holy Bible, New International Version, copyright © 1973, 1978, 1984 by International Bible Society, and are used by permission of Hodder & Stoughton Publishers, a member of the Hachette Livre UK Group. All rights reserved. 'NIV' is a registered trademark of International Bible Society. UK trademark number 1448790.

Scripture quotations taken from the New Revised Standard Version of the Bible, Anglicised Edition, copyright © 1989, 1995 by the Division of Christian Education of the National Council of the Churches of Christ in the United States of America, are used by permission. All rights reserved.

Scripture quotations taken from The Holy Bible, English Standard Version. Copyright © 2001 by Crossway Bibles, a division of Good News Publishers.

A catalogue record for this book is available from the British Library
Printed in Singapore by Craft Print International Ltd

Growing a caring church

Practical guidelines for pastoral care

Wendy Billington

This book is dedicated to my dear friends within my church family, together with Miles and Angus, the two rectors with whom I have served and who gave me the privilege of sharing in the work of pastoral care.

I am especially indebted to my special friend, Jean Watson, for the practical help and encouragement she has given me in bringing this book to fruition.

Contents

The need for pastoral care

'My command is this: Love each other as I have loved you. Greater love has no one than this, that he lay down his life for his friends.'
JOHN 15:12–13

The compassion of Jesus

The word 'pastoral' conjures up for me a picture of a shepherd gathering together his wandering flock of sheep on the hillside above the Lake of Galilee—lovingly tending, leading, protecting and nurturing them. In John 10:11, Jesus calls himself the 'good shepherd' who would lay down his life for his sheep. Accordingly, the cross, where Jesus gave his life for us in perfect obedience and with infinite compassion, should be a starting point for our pastoral care. As we survey the wonder of the cross, it should move us to show something of that divine compassion to others in both word and deed. As we turn the pages of the Gospels, reading of Jesus' earthly ministry, we are able to contemplate in wonder the love and compassion he showed to those he met who were in physical, spiritual, mental or emotional pain—and his commandment is for us to love one another as he loved us. What a privilege it is to be able to channel and communicate God's love in response to his love for us!

Having this attitude dispels any conflict of priorities we may feel between mission and pastoral care. Preaching Christ and demonstrating his love are facets of the same gospel, with words and deeds operating hand in hand. Paul tells the Colossians to clothe themselves with compassion (Colossians 3:12) as they come face to face with the pain of suffering. The hurting people we meet in our everyday lives, trapped in a variety of personal problems, are no different from those whom Jesus himself, the Colossians and others living at that time encountered. Joys and sorrows, births and deaths are part and parcel of life throughout all generations, requiring the same response of compassion and love.

Relational community

We are created to have relationships with both God and with one another. John Donne's famous line 'No man is an island' reflects the wisdom and reality of this truth. As Christians, we are in a relationship of mutual love and care for one another, and that love and care will involve us in helping one another, both spiritually and practically. We enter a relationship in which we can bring God's love and his word to nurture others. We read in Mark 2 of the paralysed man whose need moved his friends to action, so that they brought him to Jesus for forgiveness and healing. May we, too, be moved with compassion to bring a needy person to Jesus to receive his forgiveness and healing touch.

Within a home group setting, we can learn to move away from an individualistic approach to pastoral care and offer care to one another as a community of believers. I love the Greek word *koinonia*, which has no exact equivalent in the English language but can be taken to mean 'unified fellowship'. In Acts 2:42, Luke describes this community life, which the Spirit brings, when he writes that the first believers 'devoted themselves to... fellowship'.

Tackling concerns

As we enjoy *koinonia* with one another, at any one time within our groups there is likely to be someone whose life needs a bit of attention—some kind of 'needle and thread' repair. The way we tackle the repair, and with what tools, will vary according to the need. Perhaps it is helpful to see the group leader as an overseer of the repair kit, offering the various needles and threads to members of the team, to use for whatever mending task comes to light. The process of repair with the needle may be quite painful and the resultant patch a bit flawed, but it will be a lot better than the vulnerable gaping hole that it is replacing.

It is a joy and a privilege to be involved as a band of believers in such repair work, and this book is designed to encourage us not to take the soft option of ignoring a particular concern, but to develop an awareness of our members' needs and become better equipped to meet them. If a listening ear is required, we might want to address the barriers that prevent us from listening well, to improve our skills. We might also want to learn how to respond to a crisis, relationship problem or major life change in our own experience—or, when appropriate, to refer the situation to others.

Counter-productive attitudes

As we care for others, we may well come face to face with obstacles that are difficult to overcome. The Christian is as vulnerable to problems as the non-believer. Because we have a personal relationship with an all-loving God who forgives and indwells us by his Holy Spirit, we sometimes encounter a belief and expectation that we should be able to 'cope' with problems, and any failure is interpreted as stemming from a lack of faith. This attitude can exacerbate any existing difficulties. Denying that there is a problem can be another way of making things worse. Some people are afraid to admit to it because they believe they will lose credibility in the eyes of the church, so they take the easier option of continuing to act normally as a member of Christ's body, not asking for help and hoping that the problem will go away.

The home group

This book is written with leaders in mind, and particularly leaders of home groups. Maybe you are in a small church, leading the one and only home group; or, like myself, you are in a large church, leading one of many such groups; or perhaps you are a member of a cell church. The material in this book is relevant to all, irrespective of model and size. A vital role of the home group is, I believe, to apply the truth of the Bible to everyday life, enabling members to help one another to adopt a significantly different lifestyle from those encouraged by current culture and social norms. Members are also called to come alongside those who, due to their brokenness, are unable to function effectively in God's service and in response to life's demands.

As a body of believers, we all have a responsibility to encourage one another and to create a climate in which everybody can be supported, cared for and loved. These, I believe, are just some of the aspects of church and home-group ministry for all Christians, irrespective of where they may be in their own faith journey. The leader's role within the home group is to build up loving relationships between members, giving support and encouragement to them in their witness as Christians within the wider community. This ideal is not easy to achieve but, if we help one another by sharing our diversity of gifts, great things become possible and our church will grow into a loving and caring fellowship.

As we communicate God's word of forgiveness and eternal life to the people around us, Jesus, who brought healing and comfort into the lives of everyone he encountered, is our model. For our wider society to see a community of believers offering love and care to others can, in itself, be a powerful witness.

I believe that, drawing on our own times of suffering, we can bring comfort and help to others. Through my experience of a personal bereavement in my early 30s, I have a small measure of understanding for those bereaved of a loved one in their early adulthood. When faced with cancer, I began to explore Christianity and the meaning of life; and so, when I am alongside others diagnosed with life-threatening illnesses, I have confidence that God will ultimately use their suffering for good purposes in their lives. The devastating experience of a broken marriage has given me a passion for doing all I can to help people build foundations for long and lasting marriages. Although we may like to analyse the reasons behind marriage breakdown, the important issue is what we do afterwards with all the shattered pieces. Looking back on my life, at one time it resembled a house that had been bombed but not demolished, and God enabled me, with the support of friends, to restore and rebuild what had been broken down. I have accepted Christ's forgiveness and freedom from past hurts and allowed him to bring about transformation in my life. All this is a learning process, and I know I will have L-plates on until the end of my days here on earth. Throughout the learning process, I endeavour with Paul 'to be content whatever the circumstances' (Philippians 4:11).

So I offer this book as a practical tool, grounded in scripture and based on my observations and experiences, both within my own life and in my role as a pastoral worker in a relatively large church. The stories recounted do not relate to any particular individual except with his or her permission. The issues addressed are those that we might meet in any walk of life. It is with God's needle and thread, and empowered by the Holy Spirit, that we, the body of Christ, can seek to heal the brokenness in the lives of our fellow pilgrims.

Chapter 1

Centres of growth

*As apostles of Christ we could have been a burden to you, but we were
gentle among you, like a mother caring for her little children. We loved you
so much that we were delighted to share with you not only the gospel of
God but our lives as well, because you had become so dear to us.*
1 THESSALONIANS 2:6–8

Why have small groups?

Over recent years, small groups have gradually begun to play a
significant role in the life of our churches. By following the example
of the New Testament church and meeting in small groups in
homes, we are provided with an ideal setting for spiritual growth.
Indeed, Jesus himself ministered within a small group.

This book is written from a small-group perspective but the
issues addressed are relevant to us all as we share the love of Jesus
with others. Those of you who have no home group structure in
your church may feel you would like to explore ways to establish
such a structure. Some advice on this is given in the Conclusion.

I belong to a large church with around 600 members, so it is
impossible to get to know everyone. For many years, we have had
groups gathering in people's homes across our town, most of which
meet every two weeks on a Tuesday evening for two hours, with
occasional get-togethers at other times for shared meals and social
events. Churches vary in the way that their small groups are set
up: some groups are defined by age categories or by geographical
locations; some emerge from a 'Christian basics' course. Limiting
a group to between eight and twelve people enables everyone to
participate and share more easily. Thus the group provides a small
loving family to which each member has a sense of belonging and

within which all can be nurtured and built up into the body of Christ.

In my church, attending home groups is optional but encouraged. Each home group consists of 12–16 members who meet together to study the Bible, exploring its application in daily life and sharing in prayer. Our groups are considered as centres of pastoral care within the wider church, and the leaders and their deputies have the ultimate responsibility of caring for their group's members, although they may share this task with other people in the group. Each group tends to work out its own strategy within the common framework and develops a character of its own. From my own experience, I see it as essential that the home group leaders do not feel isolated and that the church provides some system of support and supervision for them.

How are the groups structured?

Our groups are centrally planned in two ways. First, the group to which we belong is selected for us by the member of clergy who has overall responsibility for all the home groups. These selections are not made by geographical criteria (that is, by where we live) but are loosely based on which church services we attend, with a few groups emerging directly from our 'Christian basics' course, which we run each term for people wanting to explore the Christian faith. Second, all the groups normally use the same study material. Some churches link their study group material with the Sunday sermons, but we don't take this route.

The groups themselves are changed every three or four years. For some members, there is relief when the life of the group ends, but for others it can be painful. Many of the leaders we appoint are commuters with demanding jobs, having to make a real effort to be home in time for the 8 o'clock start of the meeting. Families are encouraged to host the evening, enabling both partners to attend without the need for babysitters.

Many of you may have different ways of organising and running home groups, dictated by the size of your church, location, style and leadership approach. In some churches there is one group, led by the minister, who may be reluctant to hand over leadership and responsibility to others, even if they are more gifted in such ministry. We haven't necessarily got it right in my church and are the first to admit that some groups struggle. When we see God at work through his Spirit, changing lives, and when we see a deepening of relationship and love for God and each other, however, we are encouraged.

Barriers to growth

One of the barriers to a thriving home group can be a reluctance both to share doubts, fears and concerns and also to challenge and pose questions. In a group where most people are very articulate, know their Bibles well and seem to have 'got their act together' spiritually, those who are less confident and knowledgeable can be intimidated and discouraged from offering their thoughts or sharing needs. Talking with a few of the 50 per cent or more of my congregation who don't belong to a group, I have found that they are reluctant to open up to other Christians, for fear of not being listened to or understood, or of being judged and marginalised. They may well enjoy the companionship of a bridge club or social club and be able to share something of themselves in that context, but it is often on the spiritual level that they fear exposure. Whether their fears are groundless or not, these people are prevented from experiencing the joy of true Christian closeness and fellowship.

If we are prone to be judgmental ourselves, we should remember Jesus' words: 'Why do you look at the speck of sawdust in your brother's eye and pay no attention to the plank in your own eye?' (Matthew 7:3). The importance of creating an environment where each person feels at home, secure and accepted is crucial to the effective functioning of a group. At the close of each evening, each person should go away feeling affirmed and encouraged.

Another barrier to sharing may be the nature of the circumstances that people are facing in their own personal lives. It may not be easy, appropriate or right for them to share certain concerns in detail. It is vital that we respect this fact and pray regularly and consistently for individual members, whether they have been able to share openly or not. As we build an atmosphere of acceptance, greater openness and sharing may result.

Don't be intimidated by all of this! We may have a vision of a perfect home group in which each member is loved, nurtured and cared for and where everyone grows in Christ-likeness, but that situation is not going to exist in reality this side of heaven. The focus of this book is about learning ways in which we can pastor one another so that we can live more fulfilled lives and function more effectively as members of the body of Christ. I pray that you may glean something from what I have written to help achieve this objective.

We are each on a journey and have a story to tell. The springboard for this book lies in the experiences of my own journey, which you will read about in the following chapter.

Suggestions for further reflection

- Reflect on ways in which your home group can create a safe environment where each person will feel at home and accepted and will be able to grow as a Christian. Identify anyone who does not appear relaxed and work out how you can help.
- Work out ways in which you can share responsibilities within your group.
- Discuss the expectations of your group and how they are being met.

- If you don't have home groups in your church, consider approaching your minister to discuss the possibility of starting one.

Chapter 2

Journeys: my personal experiences

'Come to me, all you who are weary and burdened, and I will give you rest. Take my yoke upon you and learn from me, for I am gentle and humble in heart, and you will find rest for your souls.'
MATTHEW 11:28–29

I love journeys and enjoy the anticipation of what I might meet along the route. For 20 years I owned and ran a travel agency, and this provided me with great opportunities to journey into the unknown, sometimes on an educational trip or sometimes as a tour manager, visiting different regions of France as well as the Middle East, following in the steps of Jesus and of Paul. These were carefully planned journeys, but the unexpected could always be just around the corner. There was an elderly woman in one group who, clad in a negligee, decided to savour the warmth of the night air while sitting on her balcony near the Sea of Galilee. Suddenly the bedroom door closed and her only possible escape was via our bachelor curate's room. Then there was the gentleman whose pacemaker gave a shrill bleep as he was going through security at Cairo airport and immediate medical assistance was required. I also remember the time when I was locked up in a police station in Prague for several hours and released only when the manager of the prestigious hotel where we were staying was forced to pay a bribe.

Life is a journey into the unknown, and yet, with Jesus as our guide there is no need to be afraid, as we claim the promise he made to his disciples: 'I am with you always, to the very end of the age' (Matthew 28:20). I love the journey of life, despite the hurdles I have encountered on the way, and perhaps even because of them, for I have learned so much through them. In quite unexpected ways, God is able to use these experiences when I am alongside others, travelling a short distance with them. As I share God with them, I am enabled to empathise, to give support and to pray for them as they negotiate their own hurdles.

As I look back now on my life, I am intensely aware of the weight of the emotional baggage I have carried. Strong muscles are required to carry such baggage, and wisdom is needed both to sift and to shed what may be an encumbrance. My own load was painful at times, and I realise now more clearly that, in order to insulate myself from the pain, I developed defence strategies that involved living behind a self-created protective façade. In other words, I wanted to let others assume I was coping.

I began to learn that this façade was not healthy and that the avoidance of pain only adds to the problem. Since then, from time to time I have been forced to stop, sort out some of my load and shed the heavier items. Throughout my journey, God has been my rock, and I can echo the words of the psalmist: 'He lifted me out of the slimy pit, out of the mud and mire; he set my feet on a rock and gave me a firm place to stand' (Psalm 40:2). He not only rescued me but also used my experiences to equip me for his purposes, as you will learn as I share some of the contents of my 'suitcase'.

My faith journey started at the age of 17 when, through Madeleine, a leader in the Guide movement, I became a Christian. One very frosty November night, when other leaders and I were on an overnight hike, Madeleine sat with us around a campfire and told us about her personal relationship with Jesus and what it meant to her. Up to that time, I had found it embarrassing even to hear the name of Jesus mentioned. I later asked to visit Madeleine, which was quite an achievement for a shy person like myself, but I wanted to know more about the truth and reality of the Christian life. Within two months I had asked Jesus into my own life.

Although we rarely met after that time, Madeleine never missed sending me a Christmas card, which was always accompanied with words of encouragement for my Christian journey. I regret not having kept in close contact with her, for I needed her as my mentor, especially when life became tough.

My father had his own private and deep-rooted faith. He attended church on an occasional basis and, as a journalist on both local and national newspapers, he would happily join others in churches of any denomination in the course of his work. Deep down, he had wanted me to have a faith, so, when he was approached by a leader of a Christian organisation, suggesting that I attend a nursery group, he readily agreed. It was there, at the tender age of five, that I learned the order of the books of the Bible. I was also required to learn psalms parrot-fashion at school, but I knew little then of what Christianity was about.

Discovering a personal relationship with Jesus was life-transforming. With this newfound faith and a greater sense of self-worth, I was introduced to a church family and began to experience the love of God through Christian friends. My enthusiasm knew no bounds. I loved life in Cheltenham, where I trained as a teacher at St Mary's College. I naively chose Divinity as my main subject, which led me into conflict with my lecturer, whose theology was a little different from mine. At the same time, I was given various leadership roles, including that of presidency of the College Christian Union and others within the wider ministry of the Teachers' College Christian Union. I had a great love for God and a hunger for reading the Bible, and, after I had left St Mary's, I took the opportunity of studying at the London Bible College.

Mine was a genuine faith, but how firm were the foundations? How did my faith integrate into my psychological make-up? How strong was it to sustain me in the outside world, of which I knew very little? Time would tell me the answers to those questions. As I started on my journey of faith, I was introduced to a legalistic approach, full of dos and don'ts. 'You mustn't dibble-dabble with worldly pleasures' was one of the latter. Another was along the lines that a commitment to Christ had to be reflected in a life of purity, which excluded even a glass of wine or a visit to the cinema.

Although I was brought up to be independent, to stand on my own feet and make my own decisions, my life up to this point had been relatively protected.

When people come to faith, they bring with them their own background, together with their unique psychological make-up and the place they have reached in their emotional development. Our psychological make-up is vital to our Christian living and the two need to be entwined as we allow the Lord to transform us into the people he would have us to be. At the stage of conversion, when we are exploring our new faith, the role of our personal development may well go unattended. We perhaps don't think about picking up the threads and weaving them into our new life.

For me, it was exciting to read God's word with my new faith-focused spectacles, to receive teaching from it and then to experience the love radiating from my newfound Christian community. All this was deeply satisfying. But, as I was to become more aware later, as Christians we should not seek to become clones of one another; we need to work out most of the dos and don'ts for ourselves. We are our own person, of infinite value to our heavenly Father, who meets us where we are, warts and all, transforming us so that we can be fit for his service.

At 23, I moved away from home and, in order to be financially self-supporting in the days when teachers' salaries were insufficient for independent living, I went abroad where earnings were higher. I moved to Germany. Unfortunately, the only Christian fellowship and teaching available were in German, in which I was not fluent. A delightful German professor, a teacher in our school and a pastor of a local church, took me under his wing, but the language was my barrier and eventually I ceased attending church.

Professionally, it was a privilege to teach children of British Forces personnel in a co-educational comprehensive boarding school, situated on the shores of a beautiful lake not far from the Baltic Sea. The school was visionary in its educational approach—way ahead of its time—and had magnificent facilities. It was founded on ideals of service, character and discipline, and was a far cry from the small primary school in which I had previously taught. Staff and pupils alike lived life at a hectic pace, with sports and activities given a high profile. I was appointed to teach general subjects to the younger age group and, as an assistant housemistress, had shared responsibility for the welfare and care of the 60 girls in our house.

Gradually, during my time at this school and in subsequent years, I began to put my relationship with God on hold. The author of Hebrews writes, 'But encourage one another daily, as long as it is called Today, so that none of you may be hardened by sin's deceitfulness. We have come to share in Christ if we hold firmly till the end the confidence we had at first' (Hebrews 3:13–14). Of course God was there, but, with the lack of encouraging fellowship on which to draw, I began to falter as a Christian.

After three years in Germany, followed by a year of teaching at an English boarding school, I settled down to an interesting life in France, teaching in an International School in Fontainebleau. These were very special years for me. I enjoyed the teaching, responded well to the relaxed French way of life and developed close friendships, including one with a colleague—a classicist and Catholic, who had been educated in a seminary until he joined the army. I learned much through him and our friendship; it was rich and deep and one in which I felt totally at ease and secure. With our common love of classical music, travel, religion and art, we were in our element, Paris being just an hour away and the rest of France and Europe so accessible. Sundays were frequently spent in Paris, where we would attend church in the morning (and this could be a Greek or Russian Orthodox congregation or the British Embassy church). Then, after a leisurely lunch, we would enjoy a film or an art gallery. These days were very special.

The future that we had mapped out together was tragically snatched from us, for, shortly after we returned to England, we were confronted with his sudden life-threatening illness. Six months later, the one to whom I had grown very close died. This episode in my early adult years of both happiness and tragedy made an indelible imprint on my subsequent life. It is part of my baggage; but now, having been sifted, the preciousness of that relationship is still retained. Because I have experienced deep pain though this loss, I know something of what others go through when they lose a loved one.

It was less than four years later that I met the person with whom, at the time, I wanted to share the rest of my life, and we were married. I realise now that I entered into marriage on the rebound. I had a yearning to love and be loved and to have all my needs met in a loving and lasting relationship. At the time, I was recovering from a serious bout of depression as a result of delayed shock following my bereavement. I had only known him for five months and I didn't understand how ill-prepared I was for this lifelong commitment. There was no spiritual togetherness, no God at the centre. I did love him deeply but the marriage was thwarted by the depressive illness he suffered (it was for this reason that we didn't have children). Many years later, after exploring Christianity, my husband did make a profession of faith, but he would be the first to say that his faith was rooted in shallow soil and was short-lived. My prayer now is that he will rediscover his faith and love for God and come to experience life in all its fullness.

I always expected longevity: my parents both lived to be 93. Nine years into my marriage, I had what I thought was to be an exploratory operation on a lump in the breast (delayed by three months as my GP thought it was not serious), and I awoke to be told that I had had a mastectomy. I was given the prognosis that my chances of living beyond five years were 50/50. I felt both numb and scared when I heard the news, unable to accept the fact that my life was at stake. I loved life and was determined to conquer the cancer. At the same time, I felt challenged to dig deeper into the faith I had once had, now that the fragility of my earthly life loomed large.

This cancer episode proved to be a turning point because it made me think much more about the mysteries of life. I was intensely aware of our fallen world and the suffering of people around me—and yet, what about God's love? Where was he? I realised that I had abandoned him, but he hadn't abandoned me.

My Christian friends had not given up on me, either, and over the years had never ceased to pray for me. They were there for me at my point of need: they helped answer my questions, gave me practical support and sensitively brought my husband and me into the loving and caring fellowship of a church, where I was reconciled with God. I had many burdens to offload: those of wrongdoing, and the suffering and sadness of the years lived with God on hold. I felt like the prodigal son in Luke 15: forgiven and welcomed back into my Father's home. Rembrandt's painting of the return of the prodigal son is very special to me and is a reminder of God's mercy, comfort and unfailing love.

After 17 years of marriage, my husband left me to explore fresh pastures, and I was shattered and confused. Although my marriage had not been an easy one, I felt bereft and ill-equipped to face life alone. My teaching career had been curtailed three years previously to start a travel agency with my husband; the responsibility was daunting. There were financial commitments to be shouldered and I had little choice but to carry on with the business. Without the sense of God's presence and my friends, I would have been unlikely to survive. I built up a supportive staff team who proved invaluable, particularly when, a few years down the track, I was invited to serve as a pastoral assistant within my church and was enabled to devote two days a week to this work. Ours was a worldwide retail travel agency but over the years I began to organise and accompany groups abroad to explore the lands where Jesus himself and Paul trod. A number of people from my own church came on these tours and I have happy memories of the good times we spent together.

It was a shock when, 18 years after my first cancer episode, I developed another breast cancer—unrelated, I was told, to the first. Although it was life-threatening, this time I was less fearful, having the assurance that God was sovereign over my life and that I was secure in him, as well as having the loving support of friends. Thankfully, I made a full recovery and, a few years later, I was pleased to sell the business. Released from the stress and strain of the travel agency, I was able to divert more time to pastoral work.

I often wonder what life would have brought me if I had not gone my own way for so long, keeping God at a distance. Although I have many regrets, I do know that we have an all-forgiving God, who picks us up wherever we are in our journey and can turn our past, even with all its mistakes, into resources for future use and work. The faith I now have is more deep-rooted and I can say with Paul, 'For Christ's sake, I delight in weaknesses, in insults... in difficulties. For when I am weak, then I am strong' (2 Corinthians 12:10).

Looking back on the twists and turns of my life, I see two truths emerging. First, to those who come to faith in their student years, I would say that just as a marriage has to be worked at after the honeymoon period is over, so we have to work at our faith once we have committed ourselves to the Lord and are in relationship with him. It takes time, effort and determination to build a firm foundation for our faith, strong enough to withstand the pressures of the world. Membership of a church family plays a vital role in our Christian life and growth and should not be casually ignored.

The second point I would like to emphasise, particularly to home group leaders, is the importance of loving and caring for others, especially those who are finding the Christian life difficult or are becoming weary for whatever reason. Loving others may involve making ourselves vulnerable as leaders, so that they can be encouraged to share their struggles and doubts. God requires us to be on the lookout for people who need our help: those who are facing a terminal illness or bereavement; those who have lost their faith or are guilt-ridden and in need of forgiveness; those struggling with their prayer life or with a relationship problem or whose marriage is falling apart; business people struggling with ethical issues. Jesus invites those who are weary and heavy-laden to be yoked with him (Matthew 11:28–29). He holds out the offer of a relationship in which he walks beside us, taking on our burdens and sustaining us. With that strong presence beside us, we are able to keep going.

Suggestions for further reflection

- Identify a burden that you have carried through a stage of your journey in life and think about what action is needed.
- Read the story of Philip and the Ethiopian eunuch in Acts 8: 26–39. In the light of what you have read, describe a turning point in your spiritual journey.
- Identify someone you know who would value encouragement. Pray about possible ways in which you can offer it.

Chapter 3

Who is my neighbour?
My encounter with Dorothy

'Whatever you did for one of the least of these brothers of mine, you did for me.'
MATTHEW 25:40

Who is my neighbour? Well, here is one who might be on your or my doorstep. Dorothy, as I shall call her, crossed my path recently in the course of my own pastoral work. She was referred by her GP to our church, as she had been diagnosed with a terminal illness and it was made apparent that she wanted 'to find God'. I had the privilege of accompanying her on the last stage of her earthly journey into a living and personal faith in the Lord Jesus.

On the occasion of my first visit, there was some trepidation on both sides. I may be a pastoral assistant, but I still find that there are many times when it requires courage to visit someone. I thought I would be faced with a person who was fearful of dying, who might have all manner of difficult questions about suffering and God, heaven and hell, which I might struggle to answer. I learned from her family later that she was wary of me in case I was a Bible-basher. In fact, I found her family there in full force to protect her, but they soon retired to the garden, reassured that I was harmless.

After my first visit, God gave me real encouragement when I was told by Dorothy's eldest son, a non-believer, 'Wendy, let me tell you that your day today has been worthwhile. My mum is a different person!' His words confirmed that I should carry on with my visits and were a great inspiration to me in my pastoral ministry.

It must grieve God when we are economical with our words of encouragement to one another.

It was a privilege to spend an hour each week with Dorothy, reading with her the Bible stories that she had read as a child. Those who teach youngsters in our churches may feel discouraged if they see them turning their backs on God as they grow older, but God still has his hand on them as he did with Dorothy. At 65, she had wonderful recall of what she had been taught long ago, and it was on this foundation that we were able to build. The Ten Commandments, the Beatitudes, the parable of the prodigal son, and the accounts of Solomon, David and Jonah were all there in her memory, alongside less familiar stories. We had some deep and interesting chats prompted by her questioning mind, and we searched the scriptures together in the treasured new large-print Bible I had given her.

As the weeks unfolded, it was lovely to see the way Dorothy's relationship with Jesus began to grow. Secure in her understanding of the reality of the cross and her assurance that her sins were forgiven, she told everyone she knew where she was going. Like the Ethiopian eunuch in Acts 8, she went on her way rejoicing—in her case, straight into the arms of Jesus. It was truly exciting for me as well as for Dorothy. We don't read about the apostle Philip's feelings but no doubt he was excited by the foreign dignitary's conversion.

Dorothy ended her earthly life without pain and very much at peace, surrounded by her family. The story of my relationship with Dorothy became complete when I was asked to take the funeral service—my first. We had come a long way since that first encounter a few months earlier.

I wrote to her son and daughters at the time of Dorothy's death:

I just want you to know how much I am thinking about you all in the loss of your dear mum. In the short time I have known her I came to realise how much she loved and cared for you; she wanted the very best for you all. She and you have taught me much about the meaning and value of family. Now she has left you I trust that something of the thought and care she has invested in you, together with her newfound faith, will reap its reward in the next generations...

I believe I was given this opportunity to help someone come to faith, as well as to offer compassion and care for her as a whole person. In Dorothy's case, pastoral care and evangelism were interwoven. How well do we grasp the opportunities given to us? Are we too hesitant, assuming that evangelism is not our gift? As we live out our faith, reflecting something of Jesus' compassion to those in pain, the Spirit is at work, enabling us to care for people and point them to Jesus. We may not all be overt evangelists but, as pastoral carers, we can work hand in hand with our fellow believers who are gifted as teachers and evangelists. Together we can live out the gospel as, with the compassion of Jesus, we draw alongside people in need.

Sometimes, an incident or person becomes pivotal in our lives, as encountering Dorothy was for me within my pastoral ministry. There were many areas of need in Dorothy's life, which most of us will experience ourselves or in the lives of others we encounter at some stage along our journey: life-threatening illness, death, bereavement and faith issues, to name but a few. As God brings us the opportunities, we should ensure that we are equipped with the right tools. There are many other Dorothys with whom we may brush shoulders. They may be members of our home groups, struggling with relationship problems, bereavement or conflicts within their Christian life. They could be friends, neighbours or colleagues who, like Dorothy, are bowed down with the burdens of life but, beneath that façade, are eager to hear the good news of Jesus. Love, comfort and tender loving care may be just what are required from us to bring another person to wholeness and fullness in Christ.

We should pray that God will make us alert to those needy

people on our doorstep, some of whom may be quietly searching for God. How often do we stop and listen to hear where others are in their walk with God? We will think further about listening skills in Chapter 5.

Suggestions for further reflection

- I became a neighbour to Dorothy at a time of need, and she became one to me as I accompanied her on her journey. Identify somebody who was a neighbour in this way to you, when you were in need.
- Think of a person within your neighbourhood or workplace with whom you could start to build a bridge of friendship.

Chapter 4

Our home group 'neighbours'

'See, I am sending an angel ahead of you to guard you along the way and to bring you to the place I have prepared. Pay attention to him and listen to what he says.'
EXODUS 23:20–21

Who are our neighbours to whom we should be listening? Well, they could be a Dorothy or they could be something like the members of the fictitious home group that I shall describe in this chapter.

It's Wednesday evening and eight people have arrived to join Shaun and Laura in their home for their fortnightly home group. Eric and Elizabeth are their leaders. Within the group there is Margaret, a secondary school teacher who has recently moved into the area to take up her first teaching post after university. She is struggling with various issues, which are evident to others in the group but rarely verbalised: her job, and living on her own for the first time, without the proximity of close friends. These pressures have taken their toll and she is looking tired and strained. She is quite shy and contributes very little to the Bible study.

Laura also looks tired—her two youngsters, aged 6 and 8, can be heard squabbling upstairs—and Shaun was late home from work and is just having his supper.

Jane hasn't attended the group for a while as she has been caring for her elderly mother, who died just a month ago.

Tom and Rachel are good old faithfuls. Tom has taken early retirement and has just qualified as a Reader; Rachel is studying for a theological degree. They are deputy leaders with Eric and Elizabeth, helping to lead the Bible studies.

Then there is Joan, who has just celebrated her 90th birthday. She is somewhat hard of hearing, but her other faculties are unimpaired and she is still driving.

An occasional attender, someone for whom other members have expressed concern, is Monica. She is a single woman in her early 40s who was jilted at the age of 25, shortly before her wedding day. Her behaviour at times is disturbing. She is an attention seeker, wearing outlandish clothes and suffering from bouts of verbal diarrhoea. Within the home group she is a constant interrupter and, having prepared for the study with meticulous detail, she tries to put the rest of the group on the spot. She frequently changes her job, always justifying the reason why she needs to leave, but the group suspects that her bizarre behaviour may be to blame. They are secretly pleased when she is absent.

Within these diversities of circumstance are varieties of personality—shyness, talkativeness, dominance, reticence, exhibitionism—along with specific needs, arising from anxiety, stress, loss, loneliness and financial concerns. This home group has the potential to create a godly family, where each member can have a true sense of belonging and where, with God himself as Father, they can be bonded together as brothers and sisters. Their relationships and interactions could become a rich tapestry, with flaws but nevertheless fit for God's service. Jesus is their role model and together they learn of him, by his Holy Spirit, the ways in which they can demonstrate his love. As the members start to accept one another with all their differences, relationships are deepened. They begin to be more transparent, shedding their masks. It is then that they can bring out that much-needed 'needle and thread' to do some repair work, helping to bring one another to wholeness.

For leaders, trying to meet these needs may well be quite daunting. Our own weakness brings us face to face with Paul's experience in his relationship with the Corinthians: 'I was with you in weakness and in fear and much trembling, and my speech and my message were not in plausible words of wisdom, but in demonstration of the Spirit and of power' (1 Corinthians 2:3–4, ESV). Paul himself felt weak and inadequate but he was able to draw on God's strength and wisdom to help meet the needs of the Corinthians.

Listening to one another is at the heart of pastoral care. Through active listening, we begin to understand what is happening in each other's lives and, as we understand, we have the opportunity to play our part in the repair tasks, helping one another to grow into wholeness and maturity in Christ. Often we need to look behind what we hear, to know what is really going on. Listening is not just about words; it has many facets, and learning some of the basic listening skills can be invaluable. Jesus himself was a wonderful listener: he drew alongside individuals, helping them towards an understanding of themselves and their need for change. In the next chapter we will reflect on each of the individuals within our fictitious home group, learning how listening skills can help to address the issues that may be the stumbling blocks to growth and wholeness in their lives.

Suggestions for further reflection

- Pray for each of the members of your own home group, thanking God for them and praying for any particular needs they have shared with you and the group. Work out a diary plan for ongoing prayer.
- Identify any in your group who may need some 'needle and thread' repair. Work out who can help and how this can be done.

Chapter 5

How to listen

My dear brothers, take note of this: Everyone should be quick to listen, slow to speak and slow to become angry.
JAMES 1:19

We know that Jesus had perfect knowledge of each person he encountered, yet listening was still at the heart of his ministry. He listened to the questions of those who were hostile as well as his followers; he listened to the needs of the sick and to the distress of the disciples on the way to Emmaus (Luke 24:13–17). With his perceptive questions he was able to draw out their thoughts, struggles and needs. Within the family of our home group, an atmosphere of acceptance is needed, and this can be achieved only through our attentiveness, concern and love for one another. Being quiet and somewhat withdrawn myself, I sometimes have the feeling that people are not engaging with what I'm saying. When they do, I feel good—valued. When they don't, I can feel quite rejected. For most of us, feeling good about ourselves is important in helping us to function with confidence.

Books and training courses abound in the area of listening skills and some of you may have come across some of these books and attended some courses. I have gained many valuable insights through training as a tutor with Acorn Christian Listeners, which have helped me in my pastoral work. For the benefit of those who know little about listening skills, however, I will devote this chapter to the subject. If we learn some of the basic principles, we can adapt them for use with the people we encounter in our home groups.

The importance of love

Love is the hallmark of every Christian, stemming from our own relationship with God: 'Love each other as I have loved you,' said Jesus to his disciples (John 15:12). We are to love other believers, irrespective of how we feel about them or how difficult it may be to love them. As we communicate our love, we build up that all-important atmosphere of acceptance, so that the other person begins to relax and can share more of themselves.

Listening in its fullest sense isn't just listening to people's words; it's about listening to their lifestyle, the way they speak, their body language and their facial expressions. Listening to another person is showing them love. It is giving them time. To give another person just three minutes of our time in this way might make all the difference in enabling them to cope better with the struggles of life that they may be enduring at the time.

Why do we listen?

We want the members of our groups to feel a sense of belonging, of being part of a family. We want to rejoice with those who rejoice and weep with those who weep (Romans 12:15, NRSV). We want to support our friends as they cope with particular situations in their lives—with overwork, maybe with their faith and doubts, family concerns, pain and illness. We need to be alongside with an active listening ear.

How do we listen?

It is very important that we develop the skill of empathy. This is about seeing the world through another person's eyes, feeling how the other person's shoes pinch, experiencing a person's private world *as if* it were our own. Before starting to listen, we need to empty our minds of the concerns in our own lives so that these don't hinder the listening process. Even before I meet someone on a one-to-one basis, I often consciously try to put empathy into play and focus on the circumstances of the other person, praying for the Holy Spirit to be my helper. He or she needs to know we are listening, and this means giving our undivided attention so that we are genuinely listening with a view to understanding the other person through their words and body language. We need to listen so well that we can repeat back what we have heard accurately.

A golden rule for me is to avoid interruption: the answerphone should be on, with no temptation to answer it, and the mobile turned off. We ourselves can be the source of an interruption, with unnecessary and inane questions that stem from sheer curiosity, or remarks such as, 'Yes, that reminds me of when I was in my first teaching post', which unhelpfully shift the focus on to ourselves.

Most people who go on a listening course initially find it difficult to listen to another person without interruption. They don't find it easy just to nod their head or indicate in a non-verbal way that they are listening attentively. We may want to talk or at least to interrupt when something triggers off a thought in us that we would like to communicate. However, interruption stems the flow of thought and may act as a barrier to attentive listening.

People communicate very powerfully in non-verbal ways, through body language, tone of voice, tears and facial expression. For example, the voice of a depressed person is likely to be monotonous and their face expressionless, while an anxious person is often fidgety. If we pick up particular signs of anxiety, depression, anger or other emotional states that may give cause for concern in someone's body language, these may well be worth exploring through the listening process. However, it is important not to go overboard in this kind of discernment. I have known a very fidgety person who seems to be very much at ease with herself in everyday life and, as far as I know, doesn't suffer from anxiety.

Learning not to be embarrassed by silence is very important. Why has the flow of talk stopped? Is the person testing the waters to know whether to continue? Maybe tears are not far away and you need to communicate in some way that tears are OK. Don't break the silence by saying that you know how they must be feeling, because you don't! Have a box of tissues nearby. Consider whether the tears are a release or a cry of despair. After holding such a silence, in order to reassure the person that you have heard them and to encourage them to continue, you could summarise what you think they have communicated so far.

Not giving advice is wise in general. It is instinctive for us to want to give advice, especially when the solution appears obvious to us. If we think of Margaret, the teacher in our fictitious home group, she does not need advice. What she does need is for us to provide a climate in which she can work out for herself how to prioritise her time between work, social life, church, friends, home group and so on. 'How do you see the present situation?' may well be an appropriate question for other members to pose, to help her find some answers for herself.

To help another person to move on in their thinking, it may be useful to ask a few prompting questions. Closed questions to which somebody replies just 'yes' or 'no' are often not worth asking; using the word 'why' can sound a bit threatening and aggressive. More open questions such as 'Can you tell me about...?' are likely to encourage the flow. When someone starts to tell their story to me, it feels a bit like reading a novel: I want to know what happens next. We should remind ourselves, though, that we are there not for ourselves but for the other person; this will help to prevent us from asking questions out of sheer curiosity. This kind of listening is not about getting as much information as possible; it's about creating an atmosphere in which the other person feels free to say whatever he or she wants. When Margaret mentions, for example, that she was angry about a colleague's remark, we are face to face with her feelings, so it could be helpful to try to encourage her to enlarge on her emotion, perhaps by responding, 'You were angry?' or 'Can you tell me more about that?' To offload such feelings to an understanding person can be very therapeutic.

In the process of listening, in which the needs of the other person emerge, we start to build up a relationship—one of warmth, love and acceptance. Throughout his ministry, Jesus met many diverse individuals in their everyday lives and he had dialogues with them. He listened and asked questions so that he could hear where they were coming from in terms of their doubts, fears, pain and lifestyle, as well as in terms of their sin and the stumbling blocks in their lives. Then, reflecting on what he had heard, he stimulated their thinking and opened up options for them to lead more fulfilled lives. He drew his strength from his heavenly Father, frequently withdrawing from the crowds to pray.

In our dialogues with needy people, Jesus' model is well worth adopting as our own, however falteringly we might put it into practice. Stepping back from the noise and busyness of our lives to pray for those for whom we care should be our priority, and, if any of us lacks wisdom, we are reminded in James 1:5 that God gives generously to all who ask.

Listening to the shy and quiet person

Let's continue to think about Margaret. On the one hand, she is shy and doesn't share herself easily and, on the other, she is aware that she needs friendship and encouragement in both her Christian life and her secular work. As we listen to her shyness, we can begin to understand that it took courage on her part to join the group. On her own she might well have struggled in her faith, just as I did when I was bereft of Christian friends. The group needs to deepen relationships with her to give her a sense of belonging to a family where she is loved and cared for.

The value of listening to someone who is stressed, lonely and quiet is not to be underestimated. When Margaret comes to the group, she is noticeably tired and mentions that she still has marking to do. When someone gently asks what she did over the weekend, it transpires that although she managed to get to church, she spent much of her time catching up with work. It sounds as if she needs a break and an opportunity to open up further. An invitation for a coffee and a listening ear might well prove to be the right way forward for her. It will enable her to feel valued and, as a relationship is built up with her, she will start to sense that she is accepted as she is.

Listening to the stressed

Now what about Laura and Shaun? They too are tired and stressed but the group should probably listen to their needs differently. Within the group, they are much more open and able to articulate both the causes of their stress and the symptoms. They normally come to the morning service at church, but 90-year-old Joan, who is always on the lookout for members of the group, notices that they haven't been there for a few weeks. The leaders, Eric and Elizabeth, are a bit wary of intruding, so at the next meeting it is important for them to observe the couple more closely. What do they learn? It becomes apparent that Shaun is under considerable pressure at work. On the home group evening, he is home at 8pm, having left for work that morning at 6.30. He looks as if he hasn't been sleeping well and has bags under his eyes. However, he joins the group halfway through the Bible study and sits down with a look of relief, as if this is a place where he wants to be and can relax away from the pressures for an hour.

It also turns out that their two youngsters won't go to bed, let alone to sleep, but Shaun is leaving that for Laura to sort out and she looks close to tears. The whole family seems to be suffering from colds and Laura has backache. Shaun shares that their boys are football addicts and there is something of a conflict on Sunday between football and church.

When Eric and Elizabeth get home that evening, they jot down all the things that their listening has gleaned about the family, including the indicators of family stress: Laura's tearfulness and the fact that she has to cope on her own with the children; Shaun's tiredness and the fact that none of the family appears to be in good health. These difficulties have been communicated mainly in non-verbal ways but the message is clear: Laura and Shaun are not coping and need an escape route.

Eric and Elizabeth pray to be shown how they or others might help. It is apparent that the family would benefit from encouragement individually and as a whole. Eric and Elizabeth invite them for Sunday lunch along with another family, who have children of similar ages, and where the husband also has a high-powered job. They arrange for the two families to come together after morning service and in the afternoon, so that the kids can go off to the local recreation ground and join others there for a game of football. It works well: the menfolk even agree to meet up in town for a walk in a park at lunchtime the following week, and the mums decide to get involved in a parenting course on offer at church.

There are obviously limitations on the help that any of us can give to those who are stressed, but the local church should have resources on which people under pressure can draw. Stress comes in all shapes and sizes for all manner of reasons, but we should be alert for the warning signs and play a part in preventing it from spiralling into burnout.

Listening to the talkative and capable

Tom and Rachel rarely miss a home group. Whether they are leading or not, they come along well prepared—but Tom tends to monopolise the discussions. He ends up taking over, since he overrules any response that deviates from his own thinking. He tries to jolly Margaret along, insensitive to the stresses she is under, and invariably answering for Rachel before she has a chance to answer for herself. He has a heart of gold and there is certainly no malice in him; he is just a very talkative person with an inability to listen to anybody else. If he phones anyone, they are likely to be in conversation for longer than they would wish. The group leaders try to work out why he is like this, so that they can do something about it, since it is affecting the dynamics of the group in rather a negative way.

Eric and Elizabeth decide to get to know Tom and Rachel better, to see if they can get a glimpse into their world and find out something of what is going on. They invite them on their own for supper, and Tom and Rachel are thrilled, as being invited out is a rare occurrence for them: people don't warm to Tom and try to avoid direct contact with him. Knowing that he has no difficulty in talking and that he has had an interesting career in teaching, Eric and Elizabeth encourage him to talk about himself and his work. They become aware that Tom is hesitant to share how he came to be a science teacher, and they wonder why, as he has never shown hesitancy before. Their obvious interest in him as a person and their non-judgmental approach prompt him to open up.

Tom had originally embarked on a career in medicine but, during his final year, his father left his mother and went to live abroad, and then Tom failed his finals. From the bitter way he talks, it is clear that he has never forgiven his father for his behaviour; nor has he come to terms with the fact that he failed to pursue a career that had been his vision since he was a seven-year-old. His father left the family virtually penniless, so Tom became a breadwinner by fast-tracking into a teaching career. It would take a psychologist or trained counsellor to analyse the full implications of all this, but even Eric and Elizabeth can tell that basically Tom feels insecure and has a deep-rooted desire to prove himself. It is apparent, too, that Rachel sees her role as one of boosting his ego. Eric tentatively suggests that Tom might consider counselling. Having heard his own pain and with a new awareness of the effect it is having on his present life, Tom agrees to give it a go.

Tom is then invited to share something of his story with the group and, somewhat reluctantly, he agrees to do this. In the past, the group has found him a 'know all' and a bit of a bore. Now, as they listen, they begin to understand what lies behind his behaviour. Afterwards there is a gradual transformation in Tom's conduct at the meetings. He is no longer so talkative, with such a need to boost his ego. He shares something of his own thoughts and feelings and then graciously listens to the thoughts and concerns of others. The group has been able to listen to him and deepen their relationship with him, and so he feels loved and accepted and discovers a new sense of belonging to the group.

Insecurity and low self-esteem may not necessarily be the cause of talkativeness; whatever the reason, though, if someone's talkativeness becomes a hindrance to others, it should be gently and lovingly brought to that person's attention. Having given them an awareness of the effect their behaviour has on others, half the battle may be won.

Listening to the elderly

Despite her age and deafness, 90-year-old Joan is very astute. She is a regular at the home group and comes along with cake or biscuits that she has made. She is also a regular at the morning services and looks out for and greets members of the group. If they don't appear, she is quite likely to send them a card saying, 'We missed you on Sunday—we hope you are OK' and even follows it up with a gift of cake or flowers. Not everyone likes this intrusion, though. Joan is lonely, and this loneliness is exacerbated by her deafness as she has great difficulty in following conversations and home group discussions. The group members smile at her kindly gestures, but are they meeting her needs? Some of them decide to get to know her better so that she can be more effectively integrated into the group. As a first step, Eric and Elizabeth invite her to Sunday lunch.

Communication is obviously a barrier for those who are deaf, a disability that often results in isolation. Eric's father was deaf towards the end of his life and he has learned the importance of speaking clearly rather than loudly, which he does with Joan on that first lunchtime.

Both he and Elizabeth are amazed at how well Joan is managing her life; it is clear that she wants to be as independent as her situation will allow. She views life in a positive way, purposely trying to spend time with younger people. She talks about positive topics in preference to negative ones such as illness. She describes her experiences of being alongside a number of her friends in the closing months of their lives. Some were fearful of death and it is apparent that she has been a real comfort and strength to many over the years.

The Sunday lunch they share is a turning point in Eric and Elizabeth's understanding of elderly people. Previously they have held certain prejudices and been wary of older people, as they had once found themselves involved in an unfortunate relationship. An elderly widow in one of the groups they previously led became emotionally dependent on them to a crippling extent after the death of her husband. Due to that unexpected and difficult experience, Eric and Elizabeth tend not to seek out older people's company. They see many elderly people as demanding; others come across as boring, and there is often the problem of poor hearing, which can make group participation difficult. But Eric and Elizabeth come to see that they are dishonouring God by holding these negative attitudes towards older people rather than getting to know and understand each one as an individual.

Like Eric and Elizabeth, I used to have similar prejudices towards the elderly. Then I attended a conference on ageism, which helped to transform my negative attitudes. We are reminded by the psalmist to value the older person: 'The righteous will flourish like a palm tree, they will grow like a cedar of Lebanon... They will still bear fruit in old age, they will stay fresh and green' (Psalm 92:12, 14).

Teaching us to value the older generation may need to be higher on our church's agenda. There are many people like Joan in our churches who have no immediate family. We should encourage our leaders to adopt older people into their home groups. As we get to know them, through listening to them and giving them space to talk, we will begin to value what they are able to offer us in wisdom and experience. We will also find ways in which some of their needs, be they physical, emotional or spiritual, may be met.

Communicating with the bereaved

As co-leader of the group, Elizabeth feels guilty about her lack of care for Jane during her mother's illness and subsequent death. Jane had been fulfilling the classic role of the unmarried daughter who stays at home to care for elderly parents; the mother's death may, in fact, have been something of a relief for her. Elizabeth asks Jane to meet her for coffee one day and, when they do so, she encourages Jane to talk about her mum. The group has previously sent cards with appropriate verses of comfort, as well as flowers and books to help her through the grieving process, but no one has brought up the mother's name in conversation.

It becomes clear from the conversation that Jane needs some fun, and, in time, she is persuaded to join the drama group that sometimes performs sketches for the evening service. The group members are beginning to communicate their love for her in a way to which she can respond. Following their coffee and chat together, Elizabeth invites Jane out, and this gives her a further opportunity to hear how well Jane is now beginning to cope and come to terms with life on her own. Elizabeth finds that Jane doesn't want to talk so much about the present, or about her mother's illness or death, but rather about her life over the period of many years before her mother died. She talks about the demands her mother made on her, the resentment she felt towards her married sister who rarely visited or communicated with her mother, and her regret at not being married and having children. Listening is a way in which Elizabeth is able, in a sense, to share Jane's pain. There are tears and there are silences. Elizabeth actually says very little. Instead, she silently prays that the Holy Spirit will use her quiet listening for Jane's comfort and healing. Later, Jane writes to thank her for her help, mentions that she finds it difficult to pray, and asks if Elizabeth could help her. They arrange to meet twice a month and, as Elizabeth listens, Jane gradually unfolds the story of her journey of faith and the struggles she is currently experiencing in her Christian life.

Communicating with those who don't fit in

We all know people who don't fit in, and a number of us have them in our home groups. Some are insensitive to the needs of others and have difficulty in forming friendships. They are likely to feel rejected, frustrated and lonely.

Monica would be a misfit in any group. The group has tried to accept her as she is, but it is often difficult to remember that she is a child of God and loved by him. Most listening courses start with two powerful questions: 'What does it feel like to be listened to?' and 'What does it feel like not to be listened to?' Thinking about it, the group realise that they have not listened to Monica. They have listened to her bizarre behaviour, but never to her feelings. They don't know her as a person or see what lies behind her mask; they have assumed that she doesn't want to talk about herself in any rational way. It is worth a try, though, so Elizabeth invites her to the cinema to see *Shadowlands*, knowing that she is a fan of C.S. Lewis. It is a tear- jerking film and they both come out red-eyed.

They go for a bite to eat in a nearby restaurant and, over the meal, they begin to discuss the film in general and C.S. Lewis's bereavement in particular. Knowing only a little about Monica's experience of bereavement, Elizabeth lets her do the talking, at which Monica is a dab hand. She prays silently that the Holy Spirit will be at work as her companion speaks. Monica tells her that while she has never faced the death of someone special in her life, she has experienced something worse. Apparently the love of her life never had any intention of marrying her. She adored him but, the day before their wedding, he told her that he was already married. The psychological effect on Monica was enormous. Elizabeth realises that here is a lonely, unloved and rejected person who is unable to come to terms with what happened to her all those years before. She is cocooned in her grief and there seems no escape for her.

Elizabeth responds in four ways. As she listens to Monica's pain, she prays; she also arranges to meet regularly with her to talk and read a psalm together in which Monica can identify her own pain with that of the psalmist; she later sends her a leaflet giving details of a Christian counselling service, the one that Tom is now attending; then, knowing that Monica loves flowers, she invites her to get involved with church flower arranging. No one has asked Monica to help in this way before. She is hesitant but finally agrees; she proves keen to learn and does the job well.

After much deliberation, Monica eventually goes for counselling and, after two years, is still having fortnightly sessions. The counsellor is able to support and listen to her, helping to relieve her pain and move her forward. The home group continues to support her, too, offering hospitality, listening to her and encouraging her through the difficulties she experiences in her everyday life and walk with God. In some small measure, the group members are demonstrating God's love for her and enabling her to know that she is valued by God as his child. Perhaps others continue to judge her as a misfit, but counselling and hands of friendship within the home group alleviate her loneliness and isolation and help her to fit in and be better understood.

In this chapter we have seen how Elizabeth and Eric listen and respond to a wide variety of needy people. Motivated by the love of

Jesus and with the Holy Spirit as their helper, they notice individual struggles and want to help. They give of their time as they build bridges of trust and friendship. The listening process prompts each person to start to take responsibility for themselves. Gradually past hurts are healed and, whatever stage they were at in their walk with God, each moves forward into a closer relationship.

We may feel inadequate to help someone who is struggling with a particular problem. Giving that person the opportunity to share the problem with us, however, may well help them towards finding a solution for themselves, without the need for us to say anything. We simply need to be good listeners and, in all our listening, to stay in touch with God and open to his Spirit.

Suggestions for further reflection

- Here is a listening exercise for everyone at your home group meeting. In pairs, ask each person to share briefly something that has happened over the last week for which they would like prayer. Try to remember and recall what each person has said.
- How did Jesus listen? Identify occasions in his life when he demonstrated his ability to listen, and work out how you can use them as models in your own listening.

Chapter 6

Responding pastorally to a crisis

No, in all these things we are more than conquerors through him who loved us. For I am convinced that neither death nor life, neither angels nor demons, neither the present nor the future, nor any powers, neither height nor depth, nor anything else in all creation, will be able to separate us from the love of God that is in Christ Jesus our Lord.
ROMANS 8:37–39

A crisis can be defined as a time of difficulty or emergency that interrupts us in our everyday lives. We may get the news when we are at work, in bed or watching TV; we are unprepared. The unknown confronts us and we may not be sure whether things will get better or worse in the future. In some cases, we know that things will get worse.

Within our small groups there will undoubtedly be times when someone speaks of a crisis, whether their own or another person's. It may be work-related, or it may be a sudden death, a broken relationship or an illness.

As adults, some of us have probably developed coping techniques for a crisis, based on past experiences and our personal characteristics. Sometimes, however, the nature of the crisis is so overwhelming that the ways in which we normally cope are ineffective and we are in emotional turmoil, needing, but not always wanting, outside help.

How do we initially and instinctively respond to another's crisis? Sometimes we just want to curl up and let someone else help, or we may dismiss it as something the other person 'ought' to get over quite easily—especially if it is something we might regard as trivial in our own lives, such as a child's failed exam or a burst water tank. Every crisis situation is unique, though, and people's reactions will be determined by their circumstances, their past experiences, their personality and the precise nature of the crisis. What constitutes a crisis for one person may not necessarily be a crisis for another, so it is important to consider our response in the light of the other person's actual reaction, rather than how we think they ought to react.

Faced with another person's crisis, when we don't know what is expected of us, we should remember that prayer is the key. Paul tells us in Ephesians 6:18 to 'always keep on praying'. If appropriate, we can involve others in prayer, including our home group, whether or not they are directly involved in the crisis. Thanks to email, my own home group now has a system of quick communication between group members, and many people comment, after a crisis, on how much they felt sustained, loved and cared for by the prayer support they received.

Let's now identify some different types of crises and think about the different responses that may be apparent in the people involved, along with the different skills needed to respond to the event.

Different crises

From my own experience, I can share two examples of life-threatening situations requiring immediate action. Not long ago, I came face to face with a young woman who had taken a massive overdose of anti-depressants. I had to call an ambulance; she was rushed to hospital and, fortunately, soon recovered. In this case I realised that confidentiality was important, so I communicated what had happened only to her parents and a church leader. Secondly, my mother, at the age of 93, fell as she dropped a kettle of boiling water. She had the presence of mind to use her 'call aid', so there was the minimum of delay before help arrived.

Bereavements can also require immediate response, especially when the death has been sudden, as a result of an accident, heart attack or suicide.

Then there are crises occurring in the everyday course of life: for example, a wife learns of her husband's unfaithfulness, or a youngster is devastated at failing to get the exam grades required for their chosen university. Perhaps a young child, left alone for a few moments in the car, releases the handbrake and the mother sees the car careering across the road, through the hedge and into the garage of the house opposite. There is no serious injury but the child is taken to hospital and the family's three other children need looking after. These may not be life-threatening situations but they still require someone to respond quickly.

On a large scale, there are national crises such as the 7/7 terrorist attacks on London. Those of us living in London or the Home Counties were particularly affected by these events, fearing for our loved ones' safety. On this occasion I received a call from a wife and mother of two teenage boys, telling me that her husband worked near Aldgate in London and could well have been on the bus that was blown up. She was unable to make contact with him until many hours later; she was distraught and I felt totally helpless. I just listened and prayed with her over the phone, and eventually she linked up with other wives who were similarly fearful about their husbands' safety.

It turned out that the husband hadn't been on the bus but had witnessed the scene as he was walking along the pavement in the same street. He had withdrawn into the safe haven of a nearby hotel with others who, like him, were in a state of fear and confusion over what they had witnessed. A variety of emotions may be evident after such a trauma: concern about safety, anger, suspicion of strangers and a feeling that life is out of control. At such a time of crisis, we can find some comfort in being with those who have shared the same experience.

Different responses

An important point to make at the outset is that sometimes we need to ask another person to respond to a crisis, instead of ourselves. Perhaps we ourselves are recovering from a trauma and do not have the emotional space or energy to cope with anyone else's problems; or we might simply have enough to deal with in the busyness of our own lives, without taking on the care of anyone else.

We should also be prepared to be surprised by the coping skills that some people exhibit in a crisis that might derail others. Someone I know—I will call her Priscilla—lost her mother when she was twelve. She played a vital role in the upbringing of her family, as there were no grandparents or other relatives nearby who could help. With her father she shared the responsibility of caring for her two siblings, then aged three and six. She learned at an early age to cope with difficulties. Twenty years later, her husband was seriously injured in a road accident, and the people around her, eager to do anything to help, were amazed at how easily she took command of this life-or-death situation. She was emotionally more mature than many others of her age, as a result of the experiences in the formative years of her life. She was able to talk freely about her husband's situation. Her basic need was to release her pent-up feelings, and this she was able to do with the support of a close friend, who gave her a listening ear and shoulder on which to cry.

Others may not have the same coping techniques, however, and their emotions may be all over the place. Anxiety is likely to be very much in evidence and can affect clear thinking and decision-making. There may be outbursts of anger and anyone, even those trying to help, can end up in the firing line. Feelings of guilt can also be a common reaction, if the person believes that they have caused or contributed to the crisis. I can recall my own guilt when my elderly mother fell with that kettle of boiling water, because I had been responsible for filling it.

Different skills

Empathy is an invaluable tool for crisis situations, and I have already written about the importance of this skill in the previous chapter. Empathy means trying to understand what the other person is experiencing and feeling. It involves communicating warmth, and it shows that you care and are trying to help. There are occasions—for example, when a sudden death occurs—when empathy may come into play instinctively. I can find myself so deeply involved in another person's situation that it is a shock subsequently to realise that the crisis was not my own. This deep empathy can, in fact, be very draining. 'Jesus wept' (John 11:35) is the shortest verse in the Bible but a very moving one. Jesus cared deeply about his friends, Mary and Martha, when their brother Lazarus died: their suffering 'deeply moved' and 'troubled' him (v. 33). Although Jesus knew what he was going to do, the sight of their suffering moved him to tears.

Our empathy may be such that we struggle to think how we can help. When I was called alongside someone whose husband had died suddenly, my immediate response was one of total inadequacy. I needed to be reminded that I was not alone, that I was God's representative and he was my resource. The analogy of the vine and the branches that Jesus used comes to mind. A branch draws its vital sap from the vine to which it is joined. In the same way, we draw our vitality from Jesus: as he said to his disciples, 'apart from me you can do nothing' (John 15:5b).

As well as empathy, another vital response is being there for the person in crisis. This means showing sympathy, not by saying, 'I know how you feel' but by saying, perhaps, 'You must feel very angry' or 'That must be terrible for you!' We can even show sympathy by saying nothing at all. When Job's three friends heard about his troubles, what did they do? They left their homes and 'met together by agreement to go and sympathise with him and comfort him'. How did they do this? 'They sat on the ground with him for seven days and seven nights. No one said a word to him, because they saw how great his suffering was' (Job 2:11, 13). Job was in shock and speechless. When a person is in this initial stage of shock, we don't need to say anything; our presence communicates our sympathy and love.

As I write this, I have a card in front of me from a person recently widowed, thanking me for 'being there'. On another occasion, someone in our church lost her only daughter, who was eight months pregnant, in a road accident. When I picked up her message from my answerphone, telling me what had happened, and as I set off for her house, I felt totally inadequate. What could I possibly say to her? I cried to God for his help as I rang her doorbell. When I saw her so stricken with grief, all I could do was hug and hug and listen and listen. Maybe in some way I was able to communicate God's love and compassion.

Listening in a crisis is one of the greatest gifts we can offer. 'My dear brothers, take note of this: everyone should be quick to listen, slow to speak and slow to become angry' (James 1:19). Many of us are poor listeners in a crisis situation because we are working out what we can say instead of focusing on what is being said to us. This may be because we are afraid of saying the wrong thing or because we feel ill-equipped to deal with the situation. It is important that we listen as intensely and discerningly as we can, and with the help of the Holy Spirit. Some questions and comments require no answer or response: 'Why me?', 'I know I deserve what has happened' or 'I feel so angry with God.' We read that Job became angry with God and cursed the day of his birth (Job 3:1). Such questions and comments may need to be expressed and heard by us without our offering judgment or opinions.

It is also helpful to check out exactly what the other person has said, because we tend to interpret what we hear through our own feelings and understanding. Responses such as 'Can you tell me more about...' or 'It sounds as if...' can help to draw out the speaker's thoughts and feelings. As these are verbalised, the person begins to develop a better sense of self-awareness, and particular issues start to be clarified. They may well say, 'Things are clearer now; I know what I should do.'

It cannot be repeated too often that we need to allow the other person to talk. When the crisis involves a death or accident, we may find that the person wants to relive the story and tell it time and time again. If they don't do this spontaneously, in some cases it may be appropriate to encourage them to do so. As we have already considered in the chapter on listening, being listened to is powerful, therapeutic and a means of releasing tension and anxiety.

Home group leaders may be the first line of pastoral care, but ideally they should be able to call on the resources of the group. Practical issues may come to the fore, and home groups can meet these needs or involve others who are able to do so. A ministry of supporting and helping people in crisis is worth considering together as a group. Although it may make demands upon us—particularly in terms of time and emotions— within a group the load is spread, and the value of the ministry can be far-reaching. Prayer, Bible reading, hospitality, cooking meals, lending books, arranging lifts, child-minding or sending letters and cards can all be part of the responding agenda. If necessary, help from the wider church family may be offered. Within my own church, we are fortunate to have professionals such as lawyers, doctors, nurses and financiers who have been generous in offering themselves for consultation and have proved to be invaluable in some crisis situations.

Where does the person's faith come into all of this? Some find their relationship with God a real comfort. Others may be crying for his intervention, or angry with him, or angry and confused as a result of being told that Christians shouldn't feel the way they do. Then guilt sets in and puts a brake on the outward expression of their emotions. In such situations, I may want to turn to the psalms, reading words of comfort, reassurance and peace. Psalms 27 and 37 are wonderful psalms, expressing sentiments that people in distress can easily identify with. If they find it difficult to pray, we can reassure them of our own prayers for them.

As we care for others, we need to be resourced by God, too. We read in 2 Corinthians 1:3–4, 'Praise be to the God and Father of our Lord Jesus Christ, the Father of compassion and the God of all comfort, who comforts us in all our troubles, so that we can comfort those in any trouble with the comfort we ourselves have received from God.' The principle here is that what we are able to give depends on what we are able to receive. God is the source of our comfort. The God of compassion is right there with us and we can sense his loving arm around us; he is alongside us, just as we are alongside others. An awareness of this comfort comes from being in touch with God and in tune with his will, involving him in all that we do, because we are doing it in his name and for his purposes. When we write or say to someone, 'I'm praying for you', it may warm the heart of the other to hear it, but we should not say the words unless we are putting them into effect, perhaps there and then with a quick 'arrow prayer'.

When our late rector was diagnosed with a terminal illness, from which he died a year later, we wanted as a church family to communicate our love to him and his family; sending cards seemed a minuscule effort. We could and did pray together, and this seemed to give a greater sense of God's power than praying on our own. It developed in us a sense of unity as we empathised and showed our concern. We felt that we were working in partnership with God as we prayed for comfort, strength and the assurance of hope in the distressing situation.

Empathy, sympathy, a listening ear, being alongside, practical help, spiritual encouragement and prayer are all ways in which we can show the other person Jesus' love. The degree to which we offer support, and for how long, depends on the coping resources of the person in crisis. Sometimes professional intervention may be needed: suggesting contact with a GP would normally be the first step to take.

When the crisis is over and life has calmed down into some form of normality, we may still be needed. Keeping in touch, lending a listening ear and helping in practical ways can be a great comfort, reassuring the other person of Jesus' continual presence and unending love.

Suggestions for further reflection

- Prayer support in a crisis situation is vital. Work out how a prayer need can be quickly communicated to all the members of your home group.
- Explore ways in which, as individuals within the home group, you are able to offer practical help in a time of crisis. This could include making and delivering meals, giving lifts or looking after children, perhaps taking them to and collecting them from school.

Chapter 7

Facing a life-threatening illness and beyond

Though the fig tree does not bud and there are no grapes on the vines, though the olive crop fails and the fields produce no food, though there are no sheep in the pen and no cattle in the stalls, yet I will rejoice in the Lord, I will be joyful in God my Saviour.
HABAKKUK 3:17–18

As we journey along our own path of life from birth to death, we also travel with others, sharing the joy of new life as well as the sadness of coming to the end of life and death itself.

Recently we lost someone in my church who was very dear to many of us. We were shaken with disbelief when we heard the news that she had a terminal illness. Our hearts went out especially to her husband, her two children, both of whom were not long married, and her elderly mother. We wanted to show them how much we loved and cared for them all. Some of us, like me, had experienced serious illness and bereavement; others could only imagine what the family was going through. Together, sharing our understanding and thoughts, we were able to reach out and care in appropriate ways in that very difficult situation.

My own experience

Anyone who is given a diagnosis of cancer is likely to be shattered by the news. In the story of my own journey in Chapter 2, I mentioned that I have had two such shocks—two unrelated episodes

of cancer, of which, thankfully, I am now clear. I was facing un-
charted territory, an unknown future and my own mortality. As I
have already described, it was through the first episode of cancer
that my faith came alive again, although my abandonment of
God had included a disassociation with Christianity *per se*. At the
time of the operation, I think I was fighting God; I recall to my
shame that I even sent a well-meaning Christian hospital visitor
packing—something that has never subsequently happened to me
as a visitor!

Of course I don't believe that God sends us illness—that's part
of living in a fallen world—but I do believe that he allows it and
can use it for his purposes. Soon after my first brush with cancer,
someone suggested that I should train as a cancer care counsellor
with Cancerlink, one of a number of organisations for the support
of cancer sufferers and their relatives. This training opened the
gateway for me to develop my interest in counselling. I recall
supporting a young woman in her 20s whose mother had been
diagnosed with terminal cancer. We met together over a period of
almost a year, through the closing stage of her mother's life and into
her bereavement. I shared her emotions and pain and supported
her in the care of her mother, father and sister. When the time came
for us to part, I was confident that she would be able to continue
on her life journey, better equipped for the ups and downs that the
future would bring. I learnt much myself through this encounter
and was able to use what I had learnt when journeying with others
during the closing period of their earthly lives.

Where is God?

When people are diagnosed with a terminal illness, they often go
through a 'sorting out' time. Some may be seeking to understand
the meaning of life, while others become angry and say that they
can no longer believe in a loving God who allows us to suffer. To

some, God may seem very distant: they can't pray, and they perhaps feel guilty that this is so. We need to listen to these people with special understanding and sensitivity. Then there are those whose faith is radiant and clear for all to see. I have found it a privilege to observe people like this, to witness their faith as a stabilising factor throughout their illness and a comfort to their family and friends. Sometimes, those who are doing the caring suffer more than the person with the illness.

What about my own reaction to my cancer? Yes, I was afraid. My life was under threat—and I loved life. Events felt out of my control and my future was unpredictable. I can remember the day when I was close to a panic attack. I didn't want to die. I needed more time in this world; I needed time to live life differently. God gave me that time, through which my faith has been tested and strengthened, and I know I am now better equipped to be used in whatever way he chooses.

We can't avoid suffering but we can focus on the good that might come out of it for us and others. There may come a time when we are able to draw alongside someone else as they go through suffering, when we can use the growth that has emerged from the circumstances we endured previously.

Emotional turmoil

At such times, emotions may be very confused. Fear and anxiety are common factors. When I am in touch with someone who is feeling such emotions because they think their life might be under threat, I may share something of what I have experienced, but only if I feel that it would be helpful. Seeing me fit, healthy and content after cancer treatment could encourage some to feel hope instead of despair and panic.

Disbelief is another common response to bad news. People often think, 'There must be some mistake!' Then, when disbelief gives way to reality, they want to hang on to every glimmer of hope, such as an article in the newspaper describing a new wonder drug or detailing the success of a particular treatment. There are people, I know, who scan the internet for hours, trying to prove that their symptoms indicate some other illness and not cancer at all.

Then there are the tears, which people may prefer to hold back except in the company of family and close friends. For many, it is not easy to face others in church; and, similarly, it is not easy for other people to know what to say to them. All that the suffering person may need from us is to know that we are available to help in any way we can, and to be assured of our prayers. Others just like to carry on as usual, wanting everyone to be natural and open in conversation. I would encourage them, however, to stay in close touch with their home group and to attend the meetings if they possibly can. A small group can be a wonderful resource for support and prayer, as well as in practical ways.

When someone is diagnosed with a potentially life-threatening illness, one of the greatest strains for the patient and the family of carers is the uncertainty—not knowing the answers to any of the 'if/when/how' questions. There may be long waits ahead for the results of scans, and uncertainty about what treatment may be in store and what the side effects might be. Sufferers may have to make decisions about whether or not to accept the treatment offered, and later there may be regrets over the decision previously taken. Carers, whether they are members of the family, friends or people from church, may face the prospect of countless visits to a hospital, with the corresponding impact on their time and their home or working life.

Support

In giving much-needed support, the home group can play a vital role. Its support can be given in different ways and in many guises.

There is practical support, such as lifts to hospital, meals for the family or shopping. There is emotional support, which will be important when the person is awaiting the results of scans and tests, and also later, when they are waiting to hear whether the treatment has been successful. Phone calls can sometimes be a bit intrusive and inconvenient, and the written word may be more appropriate: a card or letter is tangible and not short-lived, the message being available for reading and rereading. I often write notes, but I sometimes forget what I have said or the Bible verse I have included, until I am reminded later how helpful it was. The weekly church news sheet might be a helpful item to give to the person concerned; other suitable gifts could include books, meals, flowers and appropriate sermons on CDs or cassettes. Even if they don't fit the bill, they do communicate that you care.

We should be sensitive about visiting while the person is in hospital: it is best to keep in touch with the family about this kind of support. It may or may not be acceptable for home group members to call in. If we do visit, we should ensure that we give the person quality time, perhaps just quietly listening and sharing items of interest, preferably sitting on a chair and not the hospital bed. The rule in hospitals these days is often 'no flowers', so a magazine or a card with a verse of scripture could be a suitable substitute. I usually read some Bible verses and pray briefly with the person, but I always ask first whether they want this and, if so, whether they have any special prayer requests. Sometimes, as they consider their prayer needs, a new line of thought may be opened and explored together.

Special touches

I would like once again to refer to Dorothy, whose story I shared in Chapter 3. The day before she died, I had a call from her family to say that she had taken a turn for the worse and to ask if I could visit. It was a warm summer's evening and I went into the garden and looked at my prize possession—a stunning red rose. I hesitated and then I picked it. I gather that the next day, when the funeral directors came for her body, the rose went too. A flower picked from your garden could mean more than a whole bunch bought from the supermarket. These little touches, which cost us no more than a brief thought, can be used by God to show something of his, and our, love and care.

For some people, there may be no healing this side of heaven, and the loved one dies. What, then, is the role of the home group? We will explore this in the next chapter, on bereavement and loss.

Suggestions for further reflection

- If you know anyone who has a serious illness, consider a simple way in which you can communicate God's love to them.
- If you were told you had only a short while to live, how could you make that time precious? Is there anything you would like to put right, such as a broken relationship?
- Consider ways in which others could help you if you, as a home group member, were faced with a life-threatening illness.

Chapter 8

Bereavement and loss

Jesus wept.
JOHN 11:35

No one can possibly understand what another person is experiencing when they lose somebody or something very precious to them. As a church family or home group, we should be there for them, but deciding the best way to help requires insight and sensitivity.

Of course there are many kinds of bereavement other than that caused by physical death—redundancy, loss of sight or hearing, amputation, loss of a spouse through marriage breakdown, loss of full health, loss of independence through old age, to name but a few. Some of these situations are covered in other chapters, too, but here I want to focus on the aspects of grief and loss that are common to all types of bereavement.

Grief before death

When we know that someone dear to us will soon die, the grieving can begin there and then, and this differs from the grief that sudden death brings. A few years ago, I was privileged to support a member of our group (I will call her Betty) who had cancer. She hadn't been in our church for very long and was growing daily in her knowledge of God: she seemed to have overtaken me already in her journey of faith. As she became physically weaker, it was obvious that Betty's desire was 'to depart and be with Christ, for that is far better' (Philippians 1:23, ESV). Seeing this, her family started to come to terms with their impending loss and the grieving began. Her husband was a believer but, for reasons known only to him, rarely attended church. He loved the Bible and was reading through it systematically. Betty was a wonderful witness to him and to those around her and he was a wonderful support to her. They were very open with each other, and in some ways they were able to share the experience of grieving together. It was not easy to see Betty's life begin to slip away, and yet she herself was so much at peace. I remember her as a loving wife and mother and a radiant Christian.

After Betty's death, as the family grieved, they were consoled by the assurance that she was now in the presence of her Lord where there was 'no more... mourning or crying or pain' (Revelation 21:4). Her husband was already some way down the path of the grieving process.

As I write this, two other older people, known well to our church family, have recently died. One was a retired missionary doctor, who was frequently described as a saint. He lost his wife a number of years ago and obviously missed her earthly presence very much. Nevertheless, he was patient and seemingly content as he awaited his own 'call to glory', as he often called it. Whenever I visited him in his residential home, I never heard a grumble from him, just quiet acceptance. I would come away with a taste of heaven as he lovingly gave me a message from God, often from a passage he had read that day. He always had his Bible with him and, even during the last few weeks of his life, he was avidly reading a biography of William Wilberforce.

The other person, we will call Ben. His wife treasured the last two years they had together, saying that they were a gift from God. His cancer was not diagnosed until it was at an advanced stage, and he had not been expected to live as long as he did. Theirs was quality time in which they grew closer to one another and to God. Although married for 45 years, they had recently attended a marriage course in our church; they often mentioned how that course had added to the quality of their closing years.

Ben stood up to the physical suffering stemming from his cancer with great courage, never complaining and with a determination to fight it. He still had work to do and it occupied him almost until the day he died. I saw him during the last week of his life, utterly at peace (he said so), resting in the faith that had been his lifelong resource and feeling excited about meeting his Maker and Lord. The scene with his family around him will be indelibly printed on my heart and mind. He wanted to die in a Christian hospice, and both he and his wife seemed to be willing him to live so that he could spend the last few hours of his life in the atmosphere of love and care provided by that hospital.

At the hour of his passing, Ben's wife let him go. As she started to accept her loss, she was able to do so with thanksgiving in her heart, as well as all the other emotions that accompany loss.

Tasks in grieving

At some stage in the life of our home group, we may all come across someone grieving for the loss of a loved one. People are sometimes hesitant in relating to such a person, for fear that they may say or do the wrong thing. What the grieving person needs, however, is a friend who draws alongside, someone who makes no demands and requires no rewards. That often means just sitting quietly with them, allowing them to talk whenever they want to and perhaps listening to the same story many times over, empathising with their pain. That is one of the greatest gifts we can offer a grieving person.

It's helpful to understand something of the grieving process. In my bereavement, I experienced shock, denial, numbness and unreality, and then depression set in. It was several years before I was able to come to terms with the loss and move into a new stage in my life. We all take different pathways through our grieving, but acceptance is an essential part of the process, bringing with it the ability to move on into some form of normality—taking a holiday, joining a club, or socialising with friends. The grieving process is not something that just happens, but a way in which the bereaved person, with the support of friends and professionals, plays an active role in working through their grief. We often hear about a grieving person 'doing very well', and this may be evident in the everyday routine of their lives—eating and sleeping well, enjoying a joke, taking an interest in everyday conversation, looking after children and so on. Alongside this, though, the person may well be working courageously through the tasks of grieving, accepting the reality of the loss and moving forward into a new future.

I have no doubt that others would have seen me 'coping well' in my bereavement. I returned to my work as a teacher, socialised and said I was fine. I was, however, reluctant to open up about my grief, for I felt as if no one would understand a loss that, for me, was overwhelming. The deep, deep void in my life and my sheer aloneness were left to fester. I soldiered on, and it was three years later that the floodgates were opened. Then, as my suppressed emotions were released, I accepted the lifeline of professional help.

Although denial is a natural part of the grieving process, it is often short-lived and gradually the bereaved person will begin to move on into reality and an acceptance of the situation. This stage is often accompanied by changing moods and even a few backward steps; emotions may include anger and guilt. To listen and encourage talking about the person who has died may be all that is required. Letting go of the loved one is part of the process of acceptance. A sign that this is happening may involve a willingness to clear the wardrobe and drawers of shoes and clothes, painful as this may be. If a person continues to be in denial, they will need love and encouragement to help them accept what has happened, work through their feelings and continue their journey towards a new life.

Those who feel utterly unable to come to terms with their loss should consider seeking professional help sooner rather than later. This may help them begin to move towards functioning at an everyday level and starting to appreciate life again. One way or another, we must allow ourselves to go through the grieving process—not to hold back the tears and press valiantly on as though nothing had happened.

Sudden death

An unexpected death happens without any emotional preparation. In some cases, the one person we really need to support us is the person who has died. The trauma can be enormous; it may delay the emotional impact and commencement of the grieving process and even the ability to deal with some of the immediate practicalities involved. What is crucially important in this situation is a friend or relative who will not be alarmed by the grieving person's changing emotional reactions but will accept them calmly and sensitively. When the sudden shock has numbed the feelings and the grieving person wants to handle practical problems themselves, they must be allowed to do so, but we should recognise that the attempt may be short-lived. We must not be surprised if the person withdraws temporarily into a trance-like state with no tears, detaching themselves from their feelings but still conscious of and valuing the reality of our presence with them.

There should be no half-truths told to a grieving person but their questions should be answered openly, however painful this may be. This will mean that, in the bewilderment of what has happened, the jigsaw can start to be put together. Normally it is wise not to protect a child from the knowledge that a member of the family has died. After telling them, gently and lovingly, they can be encouraged to continue with the routine of life. As an adult emerges from the initial shock, it is wise not to leave them alone. Their anger and fear may be so intense that they see no other escape route than that of taking their own life. If they should start to talk about suicide, it is important just to listen to them rather than panicking; we should then suggest that what they have shared with us should also be shared with their GP.

In Chapter 6, I wrote about the woman in our home group who lost her pregnant daughter in a car accident. She was initially in denial, saying time and time again, 'I don't believe it!' In a way, this denial enabled her to cope with the practicalities of the funeral and the service of thanksgiving, as well as with relating and talking to family and friends. She was able to see her daughter's body and that of her grandson, for whom she later grieved enormously, although he had lived for only a few moments after he was born. He was given a name and the funeral was for both mother and son; this was to have been our group member's first and only grandchild.

How were we possibly able to help her and her husband? By listening and just 'being there' for them, attending the funeral service (which was not in our church), and then by giving her the encouragement and practical support needed for the service of thanksgiving in our church a few weeks later, on a date that would have been her daughter's birthday. People called for brief visits, sent cards and generally showed their sympathy in various individual ways. Some four years later, she said how much she valued all that we had offered, adding that she didn't know how she would have survived without her own strong faith and our support.

Other losses

Death is the most obvious cause for grief but, within my home group in the space of a few years, we have shared several losses which have been death-like experiences. One woman in her middle years is suffering from a rare life-threatening illness that prevents her from taking part in the normal activities of life. She was in intensive care for five weeks and miraculously survived, but she is still far from well. Her growth and radiance as a Christian have been a great witness to us all. Her restricted life gives her the time she has often previously longed for, to deepen her relationship with her husband, family and friends and with God himself, as she studies and meditates on scripture and prays. When she is well enough, she will lead a home group Bible study. She loves us to pop in and visit her, and I, for one, gain much from my visits. She still has an important role, but it is different from the role she played before her loss of health. Rather, she lives her life in the belief that she has been saved for a purpose, and doesn't seem to grieve for her previous fuller life.

As you will know from the story I told in Chapter 2, I have experienced other losses in my own life: first the death of a loved one, my mastectomies, and then the loss of my husband when he left me, which had the added complexities of the pain of rejection and the fact that he is still alive. My memory of soldiering on when I was bereaved, which eventually resulted in a breakdown, prompted me to accept help and support and to draw on the resources that God provides in so many ways.

If you are a home group leader, you will almost certainly come across a couple who have had a miscarriage. It can be a devastating bereavement experience and we need to show love, understanding and support, bringing alongside an understanding person with whom they can talk about their loss. Linking them up with another couple who have had a similar experience could be appropriate. The aftermath of abortion can also bring with it intense grieving and a plethora of emotions, which may include a cry for forgiveness. Again, having a trusted friend with whom someone in this situation can cry, talk and pray can be invaluable in the healing process.

Individual reactions to experiences of loss such as redundancy or unemployment can include shock and low spirits, followed perhaps by the realisation that all is not lost. If no work is found, however, despondency may set in again. There may be a loss of self-worth, since many of us find a sense of value mainly through our employment. When we have contact with those who are no longer in paid employment, it is good for us to be alongside, offering empathy and encouragement. Again, arranging for them to meet with others in similar situations, to share and pray together, can be invaluable. We can also encourage them to structure each day. If they do not have to spend their time actively looking for a job, we could suggest that they offer themselves for some kind of voluntary work or help within the church. In these and other ways, redundancy need not be a disaster but can prove to be a time of learning, growth and new opportunities.

Spiritual help

Until the bereaved person can cope emotionally, it may not be possible for them to deal with the spiritual turmoil they are facing. Returning to church can be difficult. It may be helpful for us to pick up a grieving friend and sit at the back of the church with them, arriving late and leaving early—if the person concerned feels comfortable with this arrangement. The worship and teaching may not be very meaningful, or they may even get angry at what they hear, but it could be helpful to get back to a routine of church attendance as part of continuity and normality.

Grieving is an expression of our love for what we have lost. The greater the love, the greater can be the pain. I know people who feel that it is not right to grieve, since their loved ones are in a 'better place', but we should remember the story of Lazarus as recounted by John: Jesus showed his humanity as he wept and then demonstrated his victory over death in bringing his friend back to life (John 11).

Sometimes I am involved in a pastoral visit to a bereaved family soon after the death, as they plan the funeral, thanksgiving or cremation service. In that brief visit, I become intimately involved with people whom I may not have met before. As photos are brought out and a short history of the person's life unfolds, it's a bit like reading a novel—yet it is real, and the members of the family in front of me are in shock at their loss, just embarking on the pathway of grieving. If we belong to an Anglican parish church, our clergy will be called in to take services for those who may have little connection with any church, and this can offer many opportunities for sensitive pastoral care.

From my own experience, one such person comes to mind, who was brought up in a Baptist church but had not attended a service since her wedding, 45 years before. Now she was asking us to take her husband's funeral service. It was apparent that she was full of regrets at neglecting God over those years. Soon after the funeral, we invited her to a Sunday service and then one of our weekly fellowship meetings. In those closing years of her life, she began to experience the love of Jesus through the care, support and listening ear that she was offered. These things helped to carry her through the potential loneliness of widowhood. Her husband had been her support through life and now she was handing over her life to the Lord Jesus. She often spoke about the time when she would be reunited with her husband, and one day she asked me whether I thought her husband was actually in heaven. In response, I sensitively pointed out to her that we are not the judge of another person's heart and that our destiny is in the hands of a loving God. She seemed to understand and was reassured.

Every autumn for the last few years, my church has held a service of thanksgiving and remembrance at which those who have suffered bereavement are given an opportunity before God, with others from the church family, to remember and give thanks for their loved ones. We personally invite those whom we know have been bereaved in the last year. With Jesus alongside each of us, it is good to join together to hear his words of comfort and hope. A number of those who have attended have said how helpful and special the service has been. For some, however, bereavement is so painful that a service of this nature, especially if it is early in their grief journey, might well open the floodgates of tears, which they prefer to keep to the confines of their own private life.

Helping with loss

How can we best help people going through losses of any kind? First of all, we should be sensitive to the individual, letting them know that we are 'there' for them. This means that we mustn't 'pass by on the other side', like the priest and Levite we read about in Jesus' story of the good Samaritan (Luke 10:31–32), just because we don't know what to say. Most bereaved people want to talk not about trivialities but about their loss, and this should be encouraged. A friend who lost her husband told me that many people, aware of her enormous grief, simply avoided talking about her husband. She, however, wanted to keep the memory of that lovely, special person alive and real.

We should have some awareness of where the person might be in the grieving process and be alert to possible behaviour patterns. We mustn't be afraid of their tears, for example. It could be helpful for them to look through a photograph album with a friend or supporter present. This may well produce many tears, but also memories which they can recall with joy despite the poignancy. If I had been encouraged to cry in some of these ways after my bereavement, my story might have been very different. We might also suggest going together to a film, concert or outing somewhere, allowing life, at some levels, to go on.

Some people find it helpful to write a daily journal. It could be about what they are doing, thinking, regretting or missing— anything they want to write about, in fact. We could suggest or encourage this practice, and we could also offer help with very important practicalities, such as the sorting and disposal of clothes belonging to the loved one.

Our overall aim is to help the person to grieve in their own way and time, and come out on the other side of the experience with the lessons they have learnt—which they may be able to offer at some time in the future to others. I personally want to help people turn to Jesus and draw on his resources, but I know that I have to tread with great wisdom and sensitivity, as not everyone is as open to spiritual insights as were some of the people whose stories I have drawn on in this book. Wherever people are spiritually, though, we can pray for them and listen to God for his wisdom, sensitivity and creativity in our relationship with them.

Suggestions for further reflection

- Consider an episode in your life when you suffered a loss. In the light of your feelings and thinking at the time, what help did you receive or would like to have received? If you have not suffered a major loss, but you know someone who has, you might like to ask them to share with you along similar lines.
- Imagine that someone in your home group has been married for six years when her husband is diagnosed with leukaemia. He dies in hospital 18 months later, leaving twins who have just had their third birthday. Her parents live in Australia. In your home group, discuss ways in which individual members of the group could help in such a situation.

Chapter 9

Nurturing marriage

Jesus said, 'So they are no longer two, but one. Therefore what God has joined together, let man not separate.'
MATTHEW 19:6

In the last chapter, I mentioned a couple in my church whose last two years together had been very special, enhanced through a marriage course they attended. They had been married for 45 years! It is never too late or too soon to nurture our marriages.

I wonder what is conjured up in our minds when we think of 'nurturing'. We probably relate it to children or plants. One dictionary definition is 'providing conditions which are favourable for growth'.

Creating a garden involves some knowledge of plants, in order to provide the right conditions for their nurture; what's more, it can be hard work and time-consuming. Nurturing marriages means providing and encouraging the conditions in which the relationships and people involved can thrive and flourish. The greatest ingredients for any marriage are love, understanding and acceptance, which are God-given qualities. Those of us who are home group leaders should take up the challenge to examine our own marriages, rejoicing in their blessings but all the time working to make them stronger, richer, healthier and, above all, God-centred. In doing this, we can act as role models for our group members, encouraging those who are married to follow our example.

These words of Paul are well worth posting on the bathroom mirror and memorising, as a reminder of what true love means, so that we can relate them to our own marriage relationships:

Love is patient, love is kind. It does not envy, it does not boast, it is not proud. It is not rude, it is not self-seeking, it is not easily angered, it keeps no record of wrongs. Love does not delight in evil but rejoices with the truth. It always protects, always trusts, always hopes, always perseveres.
(1 Corinthians 13:4–7)

This particular distinctive New Testament word for 'love', *agape*, perfectly fits the person of Jesus in terms of the love he showed to those in physical, spiritual or emotional pain; but, above all, in the sacrificial love he showed on the cross as he paid the ultimate price for our forgiveness, making possible a right relationship with God himself. It is with his help that we can begin to exhibit the same *agape* love—'other-person-centred love'—in our marriages.

We are surrounded by dysfunctional families and marriages; we hear and read of them in the news every day, and they exist even within our own churches. Christians can play an important role in modelling faithful, rich and lasting marriages to the church family, the workplace and beyond. These sorts of marriages don't just happen, though. They need, first of all, good preparation at the very beginning, so that the marriage is planted in good soil; then, through careful nurturing, the relationship can flourish, blossom and bear fruit.

Marriage is precious

I see marriage as providing the deepest and most wonderful of all human relationships, but it is vulnerable to all kinds of pressures and stresses. As leaders, we need to communicate a positive awareness of the preciousness of marriage, that it ought to be treasured, cherished, nourished and not taken for granted. My marriage broke down after 18 years and, when I was left by my husband, I was devastated. Only those who have been through such an experience will know the emotions of rejection, failure, guilt and loneliness that it brings. Although much of the shine and the glitter had disappeared from our relationship by the time it ended, it was still very precious to me—something I didn't want to lose. When I met my former husband recently at a family funeral, he told me hesitantly that, if he had his time again, he would do things differently. For my part, I had married 'for better or for worse' and had sought to nurture our relationship as best as I knew how. Looking back, though, I can see how I could have done it better, which is why I now have a passion for helping couples to nurture that relationship.

I have been given a great opportunity to help with this through the Marriage Course, which a couple from our church and I (supported by a dedicated team of helpers, including cooks) run twice a year mainly for church members, using the material and resources offered by Holy Trinity, Brompton, in London. The course has snowballed and is now promoted and run in churches throughout the world. I would encourage all churches, however large or small, to consider offering such a resource both for their members and for the local community. This particular course is run on similar lines to an Alpha course and is not a difficult undertaking because there is such a wealth of material available. Sharing is completely private between each couple. Communication skills, conflict-handling, forgiveness, good sex, parents-in-law and love in action form the basis of the sessions. The course is based on Christian principles, but is non-threatening to those of other faiths or none. Having been given a taster of Christianity through the course and those running and attending it, however, participants may want to explore Christianity further, and this can done through a 'Christian basics' course.

Sadly, over the years, I have known of couples whose marriages have ended up in difficulties because they were ill-prepared in the first place. Some openly regretted ever having embarked on life together. These relationships needed a great deal of professional help if they were not to fall apart. I also knew a couple who, three days before their wedding, called it off. While, as far as I know, they had not done any kind of marriage preparation course, and their decision obviously caused a lot of upset to family and friends, I saw it as a courageous and wise action in their situation, and I know that they did not regret it.

Having myself been a victim of a failed marriage and having seen others following the same route, I am passionate about marriage preparation, whether or not the engaged couples are members of a church. If my husband and I had taken part in such a course, we would have had the opportunity to identify particular issues to work through together. As I have already mentioned, I had a deep desire to be loved and to love, and I was convinced that this desire would be met in the person I was marrying. Yet I was wearing rose-tinted spectacles that prevented me from understanding properly everything involved in the lifelong commitment of marriage. I should have known and understood more about the person I was marrying and the level of our compatibility.

One of the questions asked at the end of the marriage preparation course offered in my church is, 'Are we totally confident that the person we are marrying now is the one with whom we want to spend the rest of our life?' My rose-tinted spectacles had focused only on the short term, and the prospect of a thorny future never crossed my mind.

Building lasting love

Most people marry because they are in love. Being in love invariably manifests itself as an emotional high—an overwhelmingly exciting closeness to the other person. The so-called 'honeymoon period' characterised by this sense of being in love may last for a year or so, but, when it is over, the serious business begins of working at the marriage and building foundations so that the relationship will deepen into a rich and lasting one. This involves a love that is unconditional and sacrificial, which seeks to know and meet the other's needs.

Time together, called in some marriage courses 'marriage time', is the lifeline of any marriage and helps to keep the original sense of romance alive. This is where home groups can play a useful part in helping those who have young children. We can suggest that a couple might like to go out together on their birthdays and wedding anniversary. One idea might be to make a list of anniversary dates for each couple with children, and match it with those who are willing and available to babysit. In the marriage course we run, the reminder to have 'marriage time' is a theme running all the way through, and is a common talking point among those who have done the course. We suggest that each couple blocks out regular 'marriage time' in their diaries and ensures that it is protected, with priority over other engagements. How a couple uses this special time together is obviously up to them, but it is likely to be a meal out or a special dinner at home, or maybe a visit to the cinema or theatre. If we are in leadership positions in the church, it is up to us to be role models to other couples in terms of how we prioritise 'marriage time'.

Recognising our differences

It is important that we recognise the differences in our temperaments, personalities, backgrounds and interests, accepting them at face value and not necessarily expecting change. This is true for all relationships but especially for marriage. Many a person has entered marriage intending to work at changing what they don't like in their spouse. This route can lead to disaster, sooner rather than later.

Husbands and wives tend to lead contrasting lives during the day, so it is important to understand where each partner is coming from, and to address together any related issues that cause relationship problems. To take an example, a husband in a demanding job wants to offload his concerns when he comes home; he values a listening ear and encouragement at the end of his busy, stressful day. On the other hand, if his wife has been at home all day with small children, she wants someone to listen to *her* and give her a break from her ongoing role as mum and housekeeper. A helpful suggestion is that, before they meet in the evening, they should spend a few moments imagining being in the shoes of their spouse, reflecting on the kind of day they may have had.

Many husbands and wives come into marriage with different interests. Men often want to relax by playing or watching sport, either live or on TV, or going to the pub with friends. This, however, doesn't always go down well with their wives, whose longing is to have time together. My husband loved cricket, a game I knew little about. During my marriage, I gradually came to understand the game and enjoyed days out at county and national cricket grounds or watching matches on television. It is good to address the problem of different interests and work on a compromise together. The answer could be to develop a common interest, as I did with cricket—a game which, in the end, I came to enjoy and now miss.

Many women tend to be emotion- and relationship-centred, in contrast to many men. A wife who had been married for many years longed for her husband to say that he loved her; when she eventually verbalised this desire to him, he replied that he had told her so on their honeymoon and that nothing had changed since then. A husband should remember that his wife may need a phone call from work, communicating that she is special and enquiring how her day is going, followed by a warm hug when he arrives home. For wives, being told that they are loved and having time together with their husband (perhaps with an occasional surprise evening out or weekend away) can make a world of difference to the marriage. Being fobbed off with 'too busy' excuses can be damaging. I know someone who used to leave loving notes hidden in cupboards or drawers. This was fine until the home help found one!

Acknowledging and accepting our differences has to be a priority in building a strong marriage. When we follow this up by understanding, valuing and nurturing the differences rather than criticising them, there is a greater chance that the marriage will blossom. Identifying differences does have the potential with some couples, however, to lead to disagreement and conflict. Instead of seeing an issue as the wife's or husband's problem, it should be seen as a joint problem for which the couple need to work out a solution together.

Responding to unfavourable behaviour and conflict

Sadly, nagging, sarcasm, moodiness, lack of communication and even letting the other person down in public can be part and parcel of a marriage partnership. How we respond to being on the receiving end of this sort of behaviour is important. Do we react, perhaps unfavourably, to the behaviour, or do we try to be proactive and find out why our partner is behaving in a particular way? If there is a particular issue causing tension, we should tackle the issue rather than attacking the person. Sitting, as it were, at either end of a couch with the issue forming a barrier between us, and verbally sniping at each other over the barrier, is something to avoid at all costs. The issue must be set down on the floor between us, so that we can move towards each other to work it out together, focusing on the issue rather than the effect it is having on us. Attacking our spouse with unkind words can be very damaging and not easily forgiven and forgotten.

Forgiveness

In Ephesians 4:31–32 we read, 'Get rid of all bitterness, rage and anger... Be kind and compassionate to one another, forgiving each other, just as in Christ God forgave you.' Central to all marriages is the recognition of our responsibility to acknowledge when we hurt our spouse, to confess what we have done to God and to apologise and forgive each other. Hurt is like a big stone in the soil that affects the growth of a plant: it needs removing so that the damage can be healed and nurture can take place.

Love makes it possible to say we are sorry and opens up the way for reconciliation and communication. Within a marriage, forgiveness is very powerful, but at first it may not be a feeling; rather, it is a choice. The feeling may come later and, when it does come, it can be a very moving and liberating experience. I know of a wife who agonised for years over the fact that she hadn't told her husband of an intimate relationship she had had before they married, which had resulted in a miscarriage. This became a barrier between them and their marriage was close to breaking up. Going on a marriage enrichment weekend gave her the courage to take the risk and tell her husband. He said nothing, but, as he took her in his arms, she knew his forgiveness and experienced a wonderful release from the burden she had carried for so long. His love and understanding were amazing. As I was told this story, I thought of God's amazing love as we come to him time and time again in repentance, asking for his forgiveness.

Getting professional help

If we are aware of a marriage in trouble, it could be appropriate to put the couple in touch with Acorn Christian Listeners rather than simply suggesting a get-together with another couple to talk through an issue. A trained listening ear may be all that is needed to enable the couple to move forward. There are hidden dangers with informal types of help: the helping couple can become over-involved, getting so caught up with the problems that the stability of their own marriage can suffer; they may find themselves out of their depth with the issues and unable to provide much long-term help. If the problems are deep-rooted, it may be right to suggest that the couple seek help from a professional counselling service, such as Relate.

Your support may still be needed, however. It is sad to see a couple soldiering on in a difficult marriage, and witnessing the damaging impact it has on their children, their relationships with others and their spirituality. Our role is sensitively and diplomatically to communicate the resources available. Sometimes couples leave it too late, but I do know of one couple who, on the brink of divorce, sought the help they needed, which enabled them to overcome the obstacles and rebuild their marriage into one that is happy and fulfilled. Anne and Tony Hobbs' story is told in *Marriage Masterclass* (see the Bibliography on page 116 for further details).

Suggestions for further reflection

- If you are married, ensure that your own relationship is nurtured and that you have 'marriage time' together.
- Gary Chapman, in his book *The Five Love Languages*, suggests five ways in which we can show love to another person: time together, loving words, kindly actions, giving gifts, and physical touch. If you are married, you might like to consider which of these is the most important for you and which for your spouse, and then discuss your thoughts together. You may have a surprise! In the context of your home group, suggest one practical way in which you would like to be shown love by your group.
- List the wedding anniversaries of the married couples in your group and work out ways in which you can make these anniversaries special.

Chapter 10

Nurturing the single person

I have learned to be content whatever the circumstances.
PHILIPPIANS 4:11

In the beginning, at creation, God said that it was not good for man to be alone (Genesis 2:18). Made in his image, men and women are created for relationship—with God himself, above all. Each one of us, married and single alike, is created to love God with all our heart, mind, soul and strength, in response to his love. We are also created for relationship with other people, and this includes being in active fellowship with other Christians, whether we are married or single.

Marriage has always been God's intention, to provide companionship and sexual fulfilment and to ensure the perpetuation of the human race. Yet, within our churches, as in wider society, many people are not in a married relationship. For some, singleness could be their choice. Others might be putting off marriage in favour of a career. Then there are those who are single because of marriage breakdown or bereavement, or because they haven't married but hope to do so if it is on God's agenda for them. Not to be forgotten are those who are unlikely to be married for a variety of reasons.

God doesn't want any of us to be lonely; he wants us to know the joy of good mutual relationships. Such relationships can be experienced within marriage and the family unit and also within the warm, loving fellowship of a church family, including home groups. God is love personified, and he has given us the gift of love to channel into the lives of others.

As we saw in the previous chapter, nurturing is essential for marriage to flourish, but it is also essential for everyone's well-being. We need to work out ways of nurturing single people so that they feel fulfilled and accepted in their own right, able to play their part within society in general and the church in particular, rather than feeling in any way marginalised. As, with God's help, we learn to understand the particular challenges that single people may face, we can work to be part of the solution rather than part of the problem.

Vulnerability

Recently I chatted to a number of people in our church, men and women, who were single for a variety of reasons. I asked them if they could identify any particular problems they have experienced, due to being single. A common thread running through their answers was the fact that they are living alone, with no one immediately on hand for support and companionship. When they are unwell, there is no one to look after them; in some cases, a person can be away from church for several weeks and no one notices. They have no one to whom they can offload at the end of a working day; if they suffer a family bereavement, there may be no one close who understands; some don't attend special church functions as they don't like going on their own. Among those who have previously been married, being cut off from the person with whom they shared their life can bring a devastating form of loneliness. In my own case, I am relatively independent and cope quite well living on my own, and I have plenty of friends and company. What I miss most is having someone around with whom I feel totally at home and with whom I am able to share at a deep level.

Family

A home group can become a surrogate family, within which meaningful friendships can be formed and emotional and practical needs met. Church members should be proactive and encourage single people, irrespective of their age, to join home groups where they can be loved and supported, where non-attendance at church will be noticed, hospitality offered, and advice and help made available for the practical everyday areas of life. As a small, supportive unit, the home group can go a long way towards meeting the specific emotional and practical needs of those who are single.

When my marriage broke up and I started to come to terms with being single again, my home group became one of my life-lines. The members gave me a real sense of belonging to a family. It was suggested that we met in my home, and the youngest member of our group, just a few months old, snuggled down in my bed upstairs as we chatted and studied God's word together downstairs. Little acts of love spoke powerfully to me. I was touched when I struggled home from work one winter evening to find that a member of the group had cleared snow away from the entrance to my house.

The receiving wasn't all one-way, for I had opportunities to help others. I recall a phone call from one of the young mums, saying that her youngster was ill and she needed help; I was only too pleased to respond. As the group supported me while I came to terms with my 'aloneness', I began gradually to offer hospitality to others, inviting overstretched families for Sunday lunch or tea. My memory of that group is that it was characterised by the involvement of every member. We all cared, we shared, we prayed and we were alongside our friends at their points of need. We were 'family'.

Since then, I have been in a variety of home groups and latterly have led one myself. Each one has been very different. I have learned that when members feel comfortable, at ease and secure with one another, able to tell their own stories, both past and present, and to share hopes and fears, a true family is created which becomes one of many within the wider church.

Different life stages

Within my church, there have been hit-and-miss attempts over the years to develop a group specifically for young singles, a ministry exercised in many churches and perhaps an inheritance from earlier decades. Now there is a new emphasis on the fact that we can all live fulfilled lives, whether or not we are married. Singles do not need to be separate! Recently, a successful group has been formed for the 20s and 30s, with a healthy balance between young marrieds and singles. (We have the advantage of being a large church.) The aim of the group is to create a fellowship where God is at the centre, with the opportunity to build one another up into his faithful disciples. The members run small group meetings every fortnight for Bible study, starting with a shared meal, as many come straight from work. There are social activities and weekends away, and opportunities are provided to attend and invite their not-yet-Christian friends to a 'Christian basics' course. The downside of the success of this ministry is that our church home groups tend to be depleted of this particular age group.

When members are beyond their 20s and 30s, they are integrated into our mainstream home groups, and it is here, unfortunately, that the singles can start to feel a bit like second-class Christians compared to those who are married. The attitude can still be prevalent that people are incomplete without a mate and children. It is unhelpful to assume that a young person will one day get married as a matter of course, or to put pressure on the eligible and emotionally vulnerable by showing surprise and concern that they haven't yet found a life partner. This attitude is one with which many single people struggle. They begin to see themselves as incomplete and inferior to those who are married. Then they wonder where God is in the situation and have difficulty in understanding why they have not found a partner in life. Some end up wasting their lives by living in the future, dreaming about a suitable mate and longing for him or her to come round the corner. It is as though they are on a railway platform, waiting for a delayed train that may never come. This attitude has pressurised many people into unfortunate marriages that should never really have happened, in which they struggle to make the relationship work, feeling crippled as they endeavour to lead effective Christian lives.

Like other single people, widows and widowers may also feel that their productive life is over and that they are simply marking time. Then there are those whose marriages have ended through bereavement or divorce, who are panicked into searching for fulfilment in another relationship too soon. This behaviour is understandable but rushing into another marriage with little forethought can be a big mistake. Sadly, second marriages do not always lead to the hoped-for happy union. It is reassuring to learn from those who have been on their own for a number of years and find contentment and fulfilment in their singleness, as well as from those who do make happy and successful second marriages. We must realise, however, that neither of these situations is easily achieved or maintained.

Sharing gifts in the church family

Whether we are single or married, it is important that we receive understanding and help from others, and that we are able to offer understanding and help to others, using whatever gifts we have been given. This is an important part of belonging to the church family. In the home group, gifts can be identified, discussed, encouraged and pooled, and then used within the group itself or the wider church family and beyond. A starting point may be to ask someone to be responsible for the making of the tea or coffee at the meeting, or to help wash up. These tasks should not be seen as too menial, but as gifts of service. An older person or a married couple may appreciate the offer of a drive out for afternoon tea, morning coffee or lunch on Sunday. A single teacher in a demanding job may appreciate an evening meal before embarking on his or her paperwork.

Opportunities for practical service within the wider church setting include offering lifts to church or to hospital appointments, helping with the PA church system or producing CDs or podcasts of sermons, taking a meal to a family where someone is ill, gardening or doing a simple DIY job for an older person.

It's Saturday afternoon as I write this, and I have just been informed that a 95-year-old but still independent member of the church has had a fall, so a quick call to her home group leader should put the wheels in motion for her care—including, perhaps, taking her a meal. We can help or be helped by others, whatever our age and stage in life, whether we are married or single. For the single person who works full-time during the week, Sundays provide many opportunities for using gifts in the life of the church: helping with young people's work, stewarding and welcoming, leading intercessions, reading the lesson, playing in the music group, singing in the choir and so on.

Of course, there are other ways of helping and sharing gifts that are a bit more demanding, but each should be considered of equal worth. As Paul reminds us in 1 Corinthians 12:18: 'God has arranged the parts of the body, every one of them, just as he wanted them to be.' Paul was a gifted intellectual, a Jew and a Roman citizen, but he realised that whatever ethnic, social and intellectual differences there were between Christians, each person had an important role to play within the body of Christ. Leading a Bible study group or giving a talk involve preparation but can be an uplifting experience and a means to spiritual growth.

Just a word of warning: there is a risk that some may consider single people as having more time for 'undivided devotion to God's work', since they may not have immediate family responsibilities. This may be true in some cases, but we must not forget that many single people work full-time and run a home on their own, and thus may actually have less time to devote to ministry. There are expectations, too, that older single people, who are retired, now have time to spare in the service of others; however, they may now want time for themselves, and don't want to be under undue pressure to serve.

The early Church model

Luke paints a vivid picture of the early Church devoting itself to teaching, fellowship, the breaking of bread and prayer by the power of his Spirit, adding to their numbers daily (Acts 2:42–47). No doubt the fellowship included people of all ages, whether married, single or widowed. Within this diversity, the members expressed their love for each other in emotional and practical ways. What joy there must have been as they shared together their newfound faith in Christ!

As we get to know one another within a home group, the division between married and single people should become less significant. We may struggle with different issues but, as we share, we will find that we have much in common. If we are leaders, we should be praying for single people, that they may lead fulfilled lives whether or not they find a life partner.

We must do more than just welcome single people into our home group and church family. We must value them as equal members of the body of Christ who bring the gifts with which they have been endowed, rather than seeing them as if they were waiting for a partner to come along and 'complete' them. We should seize every opportunity to nurture all the members of God's family into maturity in Christ and, together and individually, to learn the secret of contentment.

Suggestions

- Within your home group, identify and share your gifts, pooling them and working out ways in which they can be used to serve one another.
- If you are single, how do you view yourself within your church? If you are married, how do you view the status of single people within your church?
- As a single person, identify your particular struggles. Suggest ways in which your home group or church family could help.

Chapter 11

Ministering to the older person

The righteous will flourish like a palm tree, they will grow like a cedar of Lebanon... They will still bear fruit in old age, they will stay fresh and green.
PSALM 92:12, 14

Most of us are not just apprehensive about growing old; we are afraid of it. If we are not in the first flush of youth, old age is on the horizon, and we may view it as a grimly inevitable pathway spiralling downwards. As we pass along it, faculties are lost one by one, never to be retrieved. This stage of life is poignantly and realistically described in Ecclesiastes 12:1–5:

Remember your Creator in the days of your youth... when the keepers of the house tremble, and the strong men stoop, when the grinders cease because they are few, and those looking through the windows grow dim; when the doors of the street are closed and the sound of grinding fades; when men rise up at the sound of birds, but all their songs grow faint; when men are afraid of heights and of dangers in the streets.

In Western cultures (as opposed to others, in which seniors are revered), there is an attitude of condescension towards older people, who are often the subject of jokes. They tend to be 'lumped together', generalised about, even dismissed. In my experience, though, elderly people are as different from one another as are people of other ages. There are those who continue to take an interest in and contribute to life and the people around them, irrespective of whether they are growing deaf, less mobile or whatever. Then there are others who, for various reasons, have grown to view themselves as 'old', and have become set in their ways and negative in their attitudes. This tends to isolate them from society and from the younger generation in particular. Finally, there are older people whose mental disabilities interfere with their everyday living and who therefore require specialist residential care.

The Bible's teaching is positive and constructive in its attitude to old age: wisdom and experience should be valued and respected. We read in Psalm 92:12–14, 'The righteous will flourish like a palm tree, they will grow like a cedar of Lebanon; planted in the house of the Lord, they will flourish in the courts of our God. They will still bear fruit in old age, they will stay fresh and green.' As fellow members of Christ's body, we are called to work at involving the older generation within the life of the church family, for we are all members of it. I can think of somebody in my experience who previously harboured negative attitudes but, through receiving nurture, is now blossoming, feeling valued and fulfilled despite her age. By respecting, loving and caring for older people, we can make a difference.

Integration within home groups

I believe it is very important to integrate older people into our home groups, rather than separating them into age-specific groups. It is true that many elderly people do not like venturing out in the evening, preferring the security and comfort of their own home. One answer could be to have younger people available to lead a daytime group, but, if this is not possible, there are other ways in which we can include older people, giving them a sense of belonging and spiritual support.

Within our home groups, as we have already seen, we have a ready-made family in place, designed to offer God's love through a diversity of gifts and skills. The group could adopt one or even two older people, to offer them comfort, love and support, even if the older people are not able to attend the group meetings. Such 'adoption' can pay dividends in terms of our own lives and relationships with others and with God. While older people might not be able to come along to the evening group meetings, in every other respect they could be members of the group. They could be invited, for example, to come to a home group Sunday lunch, where they would have the opportunity to get to know others and be known by others better. To aid failing memories, a list of the names of the members could be helpful—including, of course, the name of the older person themselves, thus fostering their sense of belonging.

The benefits of this kind of inclusiveness are by no means one-way. When older Christians open up and share something of themselves and their experiences, it can be enormously beneficial. Hearing about how God has been at work in and through them is very moving and rewarding for those who are at an earlier stage in life's journey.

Using appropriate sensitivity and understanding, the needs of an older person could be assessed, with the group working together to meet those needs—which will not necessarily all be practical. We must be aware that although people are frail in body, they may not be frail in mind, and it could be appropriate for a group member to visit, solely to offer conversation at a level that they are still able to enjoy. Some may be fearful about dying and need reassurance about the hope we have in Christ. Many older people, deprived of Christian friendship, have lost their way and strayed from their shepherd like lost sheep. If we don't know them well, we may be unaware of this. By drawing alongside them and building up a relationship, we can open up a way for them to share their doubts and apprehensions, and offer acceptance and reassurance.

Visiting

As different members of the group visit older individuals, we can share details of our Bible studies, read Bible passages with them, ask about their prayer requests and, with permission, share those requests with the group. We can also communicate the group's prayer requests, again with permission. In these ways, too, we can develop a sense of mutuality and belonging.

When an older person is incapacitated through frailty or illness, it is important for us to remain in touch. In such circumstances, we are bringing the church to the home through our visits. However large or small the church is, I do not see visiting as the sole responsibility of the clergy or elders of the church. It is a ministry in which we all should be involved. Visits may be on an occasional basis or they may need to be regular, with a recognised plan put in place, depending on whether the elderly person is housebound or living in a residential or nursing home. Within my own church, we normally have a frontline primary visitor, who may not necessarily do all the visiting but will keep an eye on the situation and delegate appropriately, with an awareness of the importance for time-boundaries.

When we get to know an older person better, we will no doubt identify a number of practical ways in which we can offer help. We may like to devise a rota for lifts to church and offer to sit with people during the service. We could also have a rota for shopping for them and inviting them to a meal. It could be our role, too, to ensure that they have the telephone that suits them best—whether mobile or landline—with useful numbers keyed in.

On the practical side, we should note the importance of defining boundaries clearly. A church fellowship complements the social services; it is not a substitute. It is a person's immediate family who should be responsible for alerting the GP to provide such things as domestic help, health care, meals, hearing and walking aids and so on. When there is no immediate family, however, the church family may be required to take over some of these responsibilities, as has been the case in my own church. In two particular situations, this has involved helping to move two elderly people, one into residential care and another into a nursing home.

As home group members, we have the opportunity to bridge the gaps between the young, the not-so-young and the elderly that tend to exist in our society. We can be the means of keeping older people up-to-date with church news and the ongoing life and work of the church fellowship. When they become concerned about new proposals and policies, we can consult with them and convey their opinions and suggestions to the leadership. At the same time, we can explain the reasoning behind those policies to the older people and perhaps offer our own views, too.

Dementia

In this context, it's important to say a bit about dementia, one of the symptoms of which is the inability to absorb and retain memories in the here-and-now. I have heard this state of mind likened to the feeling we have when we wake from a deep sleep, perhaps when we are away from home, and find ourselves momentarily disorientated, not knowing where we are. This could be how some older people feel all the time. For some people in this condition, we may be able to find common ground for conversation by going back to a period in the person's life that is clear in their memory. From time to time, I visit an elderly woman in a residential home who is sometimes in distress over her mother, who she thinks is still alive and currently staying in a local hotel. She cannot understand why she is prevented from meeting with her. To alleviate her anxiety, it seems best to go along with her concern and give hope for tomorrow.

I also visit a woman well known to our church family, in a home where most of the residents have memory loss. She spent many years as a missionary in Africa and is a person of high intellect who made a great contribution to the church's work through her translation of the Bible into a number of African languages. She suffers now from short-term memory loss and is partially sighted. Although she has little idea of time and place, she is quite content in her mental world, of which her son (who has lived most of his life in Africa) and family are a part, as well as her own parents—who are long deceased. We talk about each of them, and a special time for us both is when we go to her room, take out her Bible, read perhaps a psalm—she joins in with those she remembers—and pray together. She prays articulately and from the heart, particularly for her son and family. I realise that in her memory loss she may often forget to pray, but I believe she rests daily, though perhaps subconsciously, in God's promise, 'Never will I leave you; never will I forsake you' (Hebrews 13:5). As we pray together, she is given fresh comfort, reassurance and hope. She will not recall that I or others have visited her, but I know that, through the love she is given from Christians, she receives refreshment and strength. I have noticed latterly the loving way she cares for other residents, in particular those who are distressed or anxious.

A cancer diagnosis used to be whispered in fear; today we talk about it more openly, knowing that a cure is possible more often than not. Now that we are living longer, dementia is consequently on the increase. With so many negative reports in the media about dementia, it is mentioned with the same underlying fear as we used to feel about cancer. As Christians, living in the light of eternity, we should be developing a positive attitude towards dementia. Christine Dryden, diagnosed with dementia at the age of 46, in her own story of living with the disease reflects poignantly on her spirituality. I quote:

I believe that people with dementia are making an important journey from cognition, through emotion, into spirit. I've begun to realise what remains throughout this journey is what is really important, and what

disappears is unimportant. I think that if society could appreciate this, then people with dementia would be treasured and accepted.
DANCING WITH DEMENTIA (SEE BIBLIOGRAPHY FOR FULL DETAILS)

Elderly people need to grow old with dignity, supported by the love and care of others. However large or small our church fellowship, it is our responsibility to ensure that no older person is allowed to struggle in isolation during the closing period of their lives. We should remember, though, that this is something we do together, so that the relationship does not become a burden on any one person. The New Testament church ministered as a team, and home groups and churches should be adopting the same principle.

An older person's life is often like a rich tapestry of experiences, which can bring enjoyment when shared with others. Within our home group, it may be our privilege to weave the final threads of confidence, love and hope into another's life through our nurture of and love and care for them.

Suggestions for further reflection

- Identify one or two older people in your church who you feel could benefit from a partnership with a home group.
- Lay aside an hour with some of your group members to work out prayerfully a plan of action for integrating an older person into your group. Consider ways in which you can mobilise your group to draw alongside and share God's love with that person.

Chapter 12

Boundaries

But Jesus often withdrew to lonely places and prayed.
LUKE 5:16

'All things come from you and of your own have we given you': these words are often used when the offering is taken to the front of the church during our Sunday services. We associate them with financial gifts, but what about the gift of time? Our time here on earth has been given by God and we are stewards of it. We are each given 168 hours a week and, if we deduct eight hours of sleep each night (important if we are to function effectively during our waking hours), we are left with 112.

Stewarding our time

Suppose that, each Sunday, alongside our monetary offering, we were to give an account of how we had spent our time over the last week. I wonder how we would feel about what we discovered. How well do we use our time? Is the balance between work, family life, leisure and church about right, or not? Assessing these matters is not about inducing guilt but about helping us to pace ourselves and prioritise our lives in line with our personalities, callings, gifts and responsibilities.

Most of us live in a fast-moving society and our bodies and minds can only take so much. If we neglect our sleep and fail to relax, we become prone to physical illness. If we spend too much time at work or fulfilling church responsibilities, our relationship with our families may suffer. Above all, we need time to be still before God, allowing ourselves to be resourced by him. Jesus' life was a busy and demanding one and we read of many occasions when he withdrew from the crowds. In Luke 9:10 we learn that when the disciples returned from the ministry on which they had been sent, 'they reported to Jesus what they had done. Then he took them with him and they withdrew by themselves.' As we draw aside and assess the balance in our lives, we may realise that we need to make some changes and put some achievable goals in place.

In the busyness of our lives, time for home groups and other work within our church can be given either too high or too low a priority. When we think about how we allocate our time, delegation and shared ministry should be part of our agenda. We may have to decide how to prioritise God, spouse, children and church; I would suggest that putting church before God, spouse and family is not the right order.

Maintaining boundaries

If we are involved in any kind of pastoral care, we may find it difficult to maintain boundaries, however important we know them to be. There are some very practical ways in which we can help ourselves, though.

The telephone is a very convenient way of keeping in contact with people when time is limited. It is true that we can learn much about a person's situation from their body language and facial expressions. It follows that, on the phone, it is important to be alert to verbal clues, such as their tone of voice. I rarely answer the phone when I have a guest in my home or am eating a meal. If I do answer and it is inconvenient to talk, I say so and arrange a more convenient time. When necessary, I ration the time taken on a call to, say, ten minutes; I communicate this limit in a positive way to the caller at the start and keep to it. When I initiate a call, I normally ask if it is a convenient time to talk.

Money is another area in which it is important to maintain boundaries, even if we may feel that we are facing compelling need. Only last week I met a stranger in the precincts of our church who told me that he had lost a purse with £50 cash in it; he needed money to go to Maidstone, where he said he lived. I know that it is generally unwise to lend or give someone money, because it is likely that it will be spent inappropriately—for example, on cigarettes, drink or drugs—so I needed to work out another way to help him. I suggested he met me at the railway station a couple of miles away in an hour's time, where I would buy him a train ticket. He didn't turn up. It taught me a lesson that, although I want to show God's love to others, I have to avoid being conned, as I sensed I was likely to be in this case.

On another occasion, I came across someone struggling financially in a situation of debt, and I suggested a visit to the Citizens Advice Bureau for professional help. In another case, I referred someone to a caring financier, who was able to work alongside that person, helping to point out extravagances, assisting in balancing their accounts and so on. It so happens that this helper oversees a fellowship fund that we have set up within our church family—a confidential service to which members can apply in times of particular financial difficulty.

In this case, it was kinder to refer the person to a professional for this positive and productive help than to break the boundaries and give help from my own resources. There are, however, occasions within a church family when someone is struggling with a particular financial need and, out of love and concern for them, we are delighted to break the boundaries. This all requires insight and the ability to discriminate wisely.

Referrals

In Exodus 18:18 we read of Jethro's intervention in Moses' ministry, because of his concern that his son-in-law was wearing himself out. He gave Moses some wise advice about delegation and Moses changed the way he worked: 'The difficult cases they brought to Moses, but the simple ones they decided themselves' (v. 26). In our caring ministry, we must develop an ability to recognise the level of need and respond appropriately. Sometimes, as in the kind of financial difficulties mentioned above, the appropriate response is a referral to more expert help.

It's great when we can use the home group as our first port of call for someone struggling with a difficulty. To be truly helpful, though, we should remain aware that better resources may be available elsewhere for a particular person or set of circumstances.

Let's take an imaginary situation to help us think more clearly about when and how it is right to make referrals. You are a home group leader and one of your members, Tom, aged 40 with a wife and two young children, has just been made redundant. He has shared his situation with the group and you are encouraged to see that he is taking a positive attitude, confident that he will soon find another job and that his redundancy handout is sufficient to tide him over a short period without work. The group agrees to pray regularly for him and members suggest one or two jobs he can do within the church. At first, Tom seems to be enjoying a less stressful life. He has always attended home group meetings regularly and played an active part in Bible studies and discussions. Now, however, his attendance gradually becomes a bit spasmodic and, when he does attend, he is quite subdued and reluctant to talk about himself. You notice, too, that he no longer prays out loud, as he always used to.

You are concerned for Tom and suggest that he joins you one evening for a drink, to give him an opportunity to talk. When you meet, it is immediately apparent that he is in a very anxious state and he confesses that the whole situation is putting a strain on his marriage and family life. His immediate concern is about spiralling down into debt and he is in a panic about the prospect of talking this possibility through with his wife. You suggest that he makes an appointment to see the doctor, because it seems as if the stress in his life is taking its toll and medical treatment could be necessary. You ask, too, that he will allow you to introduce him to a trusted friend who may be able to give him the financial advice he needs. You ask Tom and his wife over for supper and suggest asking someone from the home group to babysit their children. His relieved face shows how much he has valued your listening ear and empathy, and so you agree to meet on a regular basis for the next couple of months.

Within our home groups and wider church family, there is great richness of gifts and experiences. While we realise that we can't do everything ourselves, we can remember that God calls people to different ministries and someone else may be better equipped than we are to help in a particular situation. A member of our pastoral care group who lost her father when he was in his early 60s says that she is available to talk with someone similarly bereaved; a mother left widowed with young children says she would appreciate meeting another woman in similar circumstances. Those who have suffered a miscarriage can find comfort in talking with someone who has been through the same experience. In our churches, we may have doctors, nurses, bankers, lawyers or financiers who are willing to lend their expertise. A person wanting to explore their faith more deeply could be encouraged to attend a course in Christian basics or to be put in touch with the clergy. The body of Christ exists for many purposes, all of which are beneficial to the individual.

As we have seen, some people may also benefit from receiving help outside the church, with referral to their GP or another health professional, or a community agency such as CAB, Relate, Age Concern, Cruse or a counselling service. We could draw up a directory of local resources and services for use among the church leadership, so that the necessary information is always to hand.

At the end of the day, though, we should always remember that our role in offering pastoral care is ultimately to encourage the people we are helping to take responsibility for their own lives and to make decisions for themselves. We mustn't act as a long-term prop for people so that they become dependent on us. Our role is to be of temporary support, enabling the person to reassess their situation and move forward, drawing on their own emotional and spiritual resources.

Confidentiality

It is a privilege to be entrusted with another's confidential secrets, but it carries a responsibility not to divulge them to others. We should always be known as people of integrity and trustworthiness.

I am aware that keeping confidences within a home group or the wider church family is not easy. We must be aware of our weaknesses in this area, however, and of any tendency we may have to gossip, and we must exercise strict discipline in relation to the keeping of confidences. I am currently helping to support someone whose marriage is under stress and is now having professional counselling. When a member of my home group expressed concern about the same person and their family at our fortnightly meeting, I was on my guard, knowing that in no way must I indicate, by word or expression, that I knew anything more than what was being mentioned.

It is wise not to encourage someone to share a confidence that could be subsequently regretted, such as in a bereavement situation; it is when a person is under pressure and emotionally charged that confidences may come tumbling out. Sharing a confidence can change a relationship. We need to ask if we are the right person to be sharing it, and to decline hearing confidences if we feel that we are not in a position to help. At the same time, we must preserve our right to consult others for advice in certain circumstances—

for example, when there are threats of suicide and allegations of abuse—as these involve issues of protection.

Maintaining a right relationship in befriending

Some years ago, I befriended and supported a woman recently widowed, and then found that a problem arose over her dependency on me, which caused me considerable stress. She became a Christian through this befriending and subsequently claimed me as her closest friend. She hung on to every word I said or had written during the period of my support of her, and showered me with presents; letters came from her almost daily. Although she never visited me uninvited or phoned me, I can recall several occasions when she waited in her car close to where I lived and, when I left the house, followed me. Once, I came home to find that she had planted a shrub in my garden. I loved the shrub but was not sure I had the same sentiment towards the one who had planted it. I couldn't shake her off, and it was my closest experience to being stalked. I found the situation difficult to handle and asked for help from a member of our clergy. Although I halted communication with her, the letters and gifts continued coming for years. The whole episode left me with a fear of overdependency and made me wary of embarking on similar befriending for some while.

Dependency can be part of the professional counselling process, but, in a more low-key pastoral care situation, there are no natural boundaries for the protection of the befriender when dependency develops. We should be alert to such vulnerability, especially if any kind of sexual attraction is apparent on either side, referring people to other agencies or getting help ourselves.

If you are meeting someone from your group on a regular basis, to help them work through a problem or concern, make sure you establish a time boundary and keep to it. The day may come, too, when you feel it is appropriate to bring the meetings to a close. If you talk it through with the person you are helping, they can be encouraged to work with you towards an ending. It could then be appropriate to encourage them to develop relationships of support and friendship from others in your home group or wider church.

We all benefit from learning when to say 'yes' and when and how to say 'no', without guilt and without feeling that we are rejecting the one for whom we are offering pastoral care. It is necessary, too, for our own protection, to take responsibility for our lives and the burdens we bear, carefully placing boundaries in the various areas of our responsibility, and maintaining these boundaries for the good of all our relationships as well as our own peace of mind.

Suggestions for further reflection

- What are the main stresses in your daily life?
- Keep a daily diary for a week to show the balance in your life between sleep, work, leisure, church, time with God and so on. You might like to do the following: draw a circle with God at the centre and divide it into agreed sectors, such as time with God, time for church (subdivided to include work such as leading a home group), marriage and family time, reading and leisure time, and sleep. Assess the result with your spouse or a trusted friend and together work out any realistic changes that should be made. Try to assess your life balance on a regular basis.
- Identify pastoral concerns in your church or home group which you are finding burdensome. Work out ways in which your burden could be lightened.

Chapter 13

Facing change

'Seek first his kingdom and his righteousness, and all these things will be given to you as well.'
MATTHEW 6:33

Here's an idea for a thought-provoking home group session: each member shares their most difficult life change, their reactions at the time to it and how their needs were met (or not). Such life changes might include starting work, getting married, having children, siblings leaving home, changes in work situations involving a house move, bereavement and retirement. All these events are common today in our culture; some we may respond well to, but others we resist.

Marriage

The early weeks and months of marriage for couples who have not previously lived together can be among life's greatest and most difficult changes. Once the wedding day and honeymoon are over, the couple, who in some cases may not actually know each other very well, are on their own with old securities left behind. They may be in love but not everything in the garden is necessarily rosy. Creating a partnership out of differing temperaments, needs and family loyalties, as well as meeting one another's sexual needs and perhaps having to balance the demands of work with running a home, is a complex business. There are hurdles to overcome and adjustments to be made if a strong and lasting relationship is to be created. For more thoughts on marriage, please look back to Chapter 9.

Parenthood

Let us consider an imaginary person whom we will call Alison, who is eager to help in some way in church. She is not unlike a number of young mums who have joined the church in recent years. She is new to the area and has attended church a couple of times, together with her husband David and two children, who are currently both under three. They like the welcoming atmosphere and Alison is keen to be more involved. Gradually her story unfolds. She has been married for four years and has moved from a large city to the small town where the church is based. Neither she nor David has moved such a distance before. David is a quantity surveyor and has just taken up a post with a building firm in London, which has a contract for the 2012 Olympics. Alison is a psychiatrist and was a lecturer in mental health issues in a large teaching hospital, having given up this job shortly before the birth of their first child. She loves her work and, in particular, her home city, where both sets of parents live, and she is not finding it easy to settle down to her new life. She has been invited to the mums and toddlers group, but doesn't feel at home there. She admits that she yearns for 'intelligent adult conversation' that is not centred around babies. Her needs have come to your attention and you arrange to meet her.

Adjusting to marriage, losing a career and having children are all major life changes and, coming so close together, they have been a bit too much for Alison. We must admire her for acknowledging her need and seeking ways of addressing it in a constructive way, rather than allowing herself to be swallowed up, as she describes it, into an abyss of despair that could spiral into depression. She is a career woman, and has considered returning to work and employing a childminder, but she wants to be there for the children and to enjoy them while they are young. With her psychiatric background, she has thought about training as a counsellor. You are aware of a short Christian foundation course for counselling skills, which would help equip her for pastoral work within the church, and you are able to put her in touch with a counsellor with whom she can talk it through.

I am aware of mums like Alison, new to our church, who are missing their careers. They don't necessarily need to work for financial reasons, but are considering it because, although they enjoy motherhood, they would also love some form of intellectual stimulation—something that a noisy mum and toddler group doesn't provide.

How else can we meet the needs of people like Alison? Some may hesitate to admit that they have a problem, even to their husbands, who may be working long hours to provide for the needs of the family. If possible, we should encourage such couples to join a home group, although this can be tricky when there are young children and a husband returning late from work. To help make it possible, we could invite them to host a group, making sure we give them good back-up support. How alert are we, also, to those who have no parents in the locality to help out with family life? Have we considered linking them up with some of our older folk, who have no grandchildren around, who can give them some support?

The empty nest

I often wonder whether it is more difficult for the present generation of parents to adjust to life when their children have fled the nest. Parents seem to have gradually become more involved in their children's education than in previous generations, following every move of the exam process and sometimes getting into a more anxious state than the youngsters themselves. This may be a generalisation, but, whether it is true or not, the empty nest is not easy. It takes courage to let our children go out into adult life and trust God to look after them. I recently met with a 25-year-old whose mother was still following her every move. This behaviour could have stemmed from a desire to protect her daughter but, more probably, it was because she felt compelled to live her life through her daughter as she was unable to face up to her own unhappiness.

When children leave home, husbands and wives may be thrown together in a way that hasn't been the case for many years. How many of us are prepared for this situation? Marriages may need some 'needle and thread' repair work at such a time, and a marriage enrichment course could be very useful to couples at this stage in their lives. We should be especially alert to the needs of a mother on her own, who may find it particularly difficult to let go of her youngsters but has to do so in order to allow them to leave without feeling guilty.

Retirement

As I've already mentioned, it was with some relief that I sold my travel agency a few years ago and entered into a new stage in my life. The responsibilities of the business were demanding and stressful, and, although I had good support from the people I employed, the buck stopped with me. Ours was a personal-touch, client-focused business and I derived a great deal of satisfaction from it, but it was frustrating when the travel arrangements did not go according to plan and clients were let down. At the time of selling the business, I was already involved with pastoral care in our church, so the transition was a relatively easy one for me: I had more time to devote to the work I loved and in which I felt used and fulfilled. For many people, however, this is not the case, and within our home groups we should be sensitive to the variety of circumstances and attitudes of our members who have reached or are approaching retirement. Loss of status and focus, less income and the prospect of decreasing energy can hit hard. We may be the ones who are able to draw alongside and assist people to manage this change, encouraging them to explore both their priorities and opportunities to develop new skills, helping them find ways to offer their gifts and time to the church and wider community.

Unplanned changes

What about changes that are not anticipated, such as a sudden bereavement or redundancy? We have considered bereavement in a previous chapter; I personally have not lived in a depressed area where redundancy and unemployment are the norm, but the credit crunch has begun to have an impact as I write. I live in a relatively affluent, middle-class town, so the redundant person I encounter here is likely to be a city worker with a large mortgage and a family used to foreign holidays, whose children attend private school. Families like this may be generous givers to their extended families, charities and the church. For some, the financial aspect of job loss may not be too severe, with the prospect of another job in the pipeline, but for others the loss of income may be shattering, quite apart from the effect on their morale and self-esteem. Putting in place a support group for those in redundancy, where they are able to share some of their concerns, encourage one another and pray together, could be worth considering.

Changes, whether preventable or unforeseen, can threaten our comfort zones and upset the equilibrium of our lives. To resist change can be dangerous or pointless; to develop a positive attitude can reap dividends. If we draw on God's resources, trusting God and praying for grace and acceptance, we will find it easier to adapt to the change. I recall a very loving and committed Christian couple who moved from the West Country to our commuter-belt town. The wife was devastated by leaving everything that had been familiar to her, including the home where they had brought up their four children. They loved their home church, where they had been involved for many years, contributing to the fellowship and forming deep friendships within it. The wife knew that she had to accept the change but was unable to come to terms with it. Eventually, through the love and care of our church and opportunities to form new friendships, she was able to settle down into her new environment.

When facing up to a change in our life, the tendency is for the negatives to dominate our thinking. Instead we should trust in our unchanging God, knowing 'that in all things God works for the good of those who love him, who have been called according to his purpose' (Romans 8:28), praying that we can accept and cope with the change and that God will bring blessing through it.

Suggestions for further reflection

- With Romans 8:28 in mind, encourage a few members of your home group to talk about any particular changes they have recently experienced.
- Identify a major change in your own life. Explore (a) what you have lost or are missing, (b) what you have not lost, and (c) what you have gained or are gaining.

✛

Conclusion

When Paul said goodbye to the elders of Ephesus, they all wept as they embraced and kissed him (Acts 20:36–37). A wonderful bond had developed in just two or three years between Paul and these Ephesian pastors, which shows us the strength of true Christian fellowship. As we read Paul's farewell and closing words as recounted by Luke in this chapter, we are in no doubt as to how this close affection came about, not least because of the quality of Paul's own life.

Caring for our fellow Christians should be our priority (1 Peter 2:17). To see Christians genuinely 'devoted to one another in brotherly love' (Romans 12:10) is a very powerful witness to the outside world.

To those who have no home groups, or have one or two that may not be functioning very effectively, I want to stress that they should not feel daunted or frustrated by what they read in this book. I would like to offer help and encouragement by telling the story of the growth of home groups within a small English country parish, showing how a vision can become a reality.

Eight years ago there were just two home groups in this church: one was run by the vicar, the other by a retired headmistress. The 20 group members were drawn from the parish and a local Methodist church, but they were tired and struggling and required an injection of new life. Today there are five thriving groups, with a total membership of 50. These groups had a small beginning, evolving from the Lent course held each year. The course participants began to get to know one another, enjoyed the teaching and were disappointed when it all came to an abrupt end with Easter. So it was suggested that they continue to meet together as a group to explore the Christian faith further through an Alpha course. The response was positive and exciting and, with the help of a retired minister who had recently moved into the area, Alpha was launched for the first time in that village with its population of less than 3000.

These people were not very familiar with the Bible and so, at the end of Alpha, which was greatly enjoyed and valued, they agreed to become a home group and go on studying the Bible together. The members developed a sense of belonging and caring; they felt secure and it didn't seem to matter that their Bible knowledge was limited. They were just eager to learn more. Others in the church began to show interest and the members started to invite their friends. With increased numbers, the group was not working quite as effectively as it had done, so another group was formed, with a few of the original group volunteering to join.

From that small beginning, the home groups snowballed. Finding new leaders was initially a problem but the participants knew that this was a work of God and that he would provide. Members who were growing as Christians were identified and approached. These people would never previously have seen themselves in a leadership role, but, through encouragement and training, they gained confidence. God has richly blessed them—and used them to bless others.

Let us recall the small beginnings of Peter's ministry. He was a simple, 'unschooled' (Acts 4:13) fisherman, working and living by the Lake of Galilee, called by Jesus to be one of his first disciples. Four years later, Peter became the chief among the apostles, preaching the first Spirit-filled Christian sermon, with 3000 being converted (Acts 2:41). God works his purposes out, often through small beginnings and using seemingly insignificant people. What happened after Pentecost is vividly described by Luke in Acts 2: 42–47. We read that the believers continued to meet together in the temple courts, but they also met in homes. There they broke bread (probably the start of a larger meal), they prayed, and in practical ways they showed love to each other. This is a model that, with the help of God's Spirit, we can make our own.

If your situation is such that you would like to explore ways of developing small groups within your church, I would suggest that you prayerfully consider how your ideas could be implemented, asking for God's wisdom and guidance. The way forward may be to approach your church leader to discuss your vision. Oversight of a church, whatever its size, is not easy; it can bring loneliness and stress, not least stemming from the high expectations of some congregations—sometimes the expectation that the leaders should be doing everything themselves. Your prayerful, sensitive approach may be just the encouragement that is needed and could be an answer to the leader's own vision and prayers.

As we come to the end of this book, here are two thoughts to take away for reflection. First, as we seek healing and wholeness in others, we should never forget that it is a shared ministry, and we don't have to do everything ourselves. Second, this ministry is shared with God. We are serving God in his church and he is there to equip us; his love for us is our motivation to love and care for others.

⋮

Resources

Christian Listeners
Acorn Christian Healing Foundation
Whitehill Chase
High Street
Borden
Hants
GU35 0AP
www.acornchristian.org

Age Concern
Astral House
1268 London Road
London
SW16 4ER
www.ageconcern.org.uk

Relate (formerly Marriage Guidance)
www.relate.org.uk

Cruse Bereavement Care
PO Box 800
Surrey
TW9 1RG
www.crusebereavementcare.org.uk

Holy Trinity Brompton *(for marriage preparation and marriage enrichment courses)*
Brompton Road
London
SW7 1JA
www.htb.org.uk

Macmillan Cancer Support
89 Albert Embankment
London
SE1 7UD
www.macmillan.org.uk

Care for the Family
Garth Road
Leon Avenue
Cardiff
CF15 7RG
www.careforthefamily.org.uk

Association of Christian Counsellors
29 Momus Boulevard
Coventy
CV2 5NA
www.acc-uk.org

Pilgrim Homes
175 Tower Bridge Road
London
SE1 2AL
www.pilgrimhomes.org.uk

❖

Bibliography

Anne Long, *Listening* (DLT, 1990)

Michael Mitton, *A Heart to Listen: Learning to become a listening person* (BRF, 2004; new edition due 2010)

Tony Lake, *Living with Grief* (Sheldon Press, 1984)

Jean Watson, *Bible Readings for Special Times: Bereavement* (BRF, 2005)

Frank Parkinson, *Coping with Post-Trauma Stress* (Sheldon Press, 2000)

Nicky and Sila Lee, *The Marriage Book* (Alpha International, 2009)

Gary Chapman, *The Five Love Languages: How to express heartfelt commitment to your mate* (Northfield, 1995)

Anne and Tony Hobbs, *Marriage Masterclass: An interactive resource about overcoming obstacles to a great marriage* (Authentic Lifestyle, 2002)

Harry Benson, *Mentoring Marriages* (Monarch, 2005)

Al Hsu, *The Single Issue* (IVP, 1998)

Christine Dryden, *Dancing with Dementia: My story of living positively with dementia* (Jessica Kingsley, 2005)

Ann Benton, *If It's Not Too Much Trouble: The challenge of the aged parent* (Christian Focus, 2007)

Agnes Whitaker (ed.), *All in the End Is Harvest: An anthology for those who grieve* (DLT, 1984)

Jerry Sittser, *A Grace Disguised: How the soul grows through loss* (Zondervan, 2005)

A Heart to Listen

Learning to become a listening person

Michael Mitton

Listening has become a lost art in our world, which has grown ever noisier, more superficial and stressed. We forget about listening not only to others but to God, to ourselves, to our communities—and even to the needs of our planet. If we do not listen, we cannot hope to grow in wisdom, to deepen relationships with others, or to share our faith in sensitive and appropriate ways.

This new edition of *A Heart to Listen* explores how, with God's help, we can relearn the essential art of listening. Michael Mitton interweaves biblical reflection with insights from many years of listening ministry in the UK and abroad. To speak to heart as well as head, he concludes each chapter with an episode from a creative story that tells of people listening and learning from one another in a challenging cross-cultural setting.

ISBN 978 1 84101 747 1   £8.99
Available from your local Christian bookshop or, in case of difficulty, direct from BRF using the order form on page 119.

Also from BRF

Bible readings for special times

Bereavement

Jean Watson

What does bereavement feel like? What helps us endure the dark days? How can we grieve so as to be comforted and, in our own way, recover and create a new life for ourselves? This booklet of 24 short Bible readings is for all who are going through such times, as well as those wanting to support others who are bereaved.

Jean Watson has written devotional books and biographies as well as books and teaching material for children. Her writing on bereavement is influenced by the unexpected death of her husband after 32 years of marriage.

ISBN 978 1 84101 418 0   £2.50
Available from your local Christian bookshop or, in case of difficulty, direct from BRF using the order form on page 119.